ROBERT MITCHUM

David Downing

W.H. ALLEN · LONDON

COMET

791·43 MiT

Copyright © David Downing 1985

Typeset in Plantin by
Phoenix Photosetting, Chatham
Printed and bound in Great Britain by
Mackays of Chatham Ltd, Kent
for the Publishers W. H. Allen & Co. PLC
44 Hill Street, London W1X 8LB

ISBN 0 491 03204 8 (W.H. Allen hardcover edition)
ISBN 0 86379 034 8 (Comet Books softcover edition)

All the pictures included in this
book are reproduced courtesy of Kobal.

ROBERT MITCHUM

Contents

1 A Promising Public Nuisance   7

2 From Henchman to Hero   23

3 The Gullible Galahad   43

4 Problems, Problems   63

5 The Straining Bodice as Art   83

6 The Country Privy   109

7 Me Tarzan, You Gorilla   139

8 Knight in Shabby Raincoat   159

9 Tequila Twilight   185

Filmography   203

1 A Promising Public Nuisance

Mitchum *(second from left)* in *We've Never Been Licked* made in 1943

Border Patrol, 1943

'Hey, who the fuck are you – Sigmund Freud?'

(Mitchum to analytically-minded interviewer, 1983)

'I LEARNED early in life that by telling a story more colourful than the truth, the truth would be let alone,' Robert Mitchum told a reporter in 1956. Many of his statements over the years, he admitted, had been 'smokescreens', designed to allow him to follow his own course 'without exposing it'.

Such an admission, though thoroughly understandable, is hardly grist to the biographer's dubious mill, particularly as regards the star's early years. There was no journalistic watch being kept on the young Robert as he attended school, or, for that matter, played truant from it. Almost all the information we have of these years comes from Mitchum himself, and separating the truth from the 'smokescreens' is well-nigh impossible. That said, it does seem indisputable that his childhood and adolescent years were neither ordinary nor easy.

He was born in Charleston, South Carolina on 6 August 1917 to parents of fascinatingly mixed origins. His father James Mitchum, the son of a Celtic man and a Blackfoot woman, was killed when Robert was only eighteen months old, crushed to death in a railway accident whilst on military service. His mother Anne, born in Oslo of Norwegian parents, was left to bring up Robert, his older sister Julie and his as-yet unborn younger brother John on the inadequate compensation money provided by the government.

She took the family back to her American home-town, Bridgeport, Connecticut, and there got work on the local newspaper, leaving the children in the care of their maternal grandmother during working-hours. They eventually attended the McKinley Grammar School, where young Robert swiftly developed the no-nonsense attitude to authority which has characterised his life and career.

He later said that he had no recollections of his dead father, 'except for a faded photographic memory', but he admitted to being 'jealous of boys who talked about their dads taking them fishing or camping and teaching them how to play ball'. Like many fatherless boys he seems to have been a bewildering mixture of the adult and the child, both younger and older than his actual years. His experience made him both independent and introverted, more at ease with the world than he was with himself. Running away from home at the age of seven certainly expressed courage and naïvety in equal measures.

He soon acquired a stepfather, though how soon remains a matter of dispute. In Tomkies' biography *The Robert Mitchum Story*, and in all previous reports, it is stated that his mother remarried only once, to the Englishman Hugh Cunningham-Morris in 1927. But in the *Rolling Stone* interview published in 1983, it is claimed that she married a newspaperman, Bill Clancy, years earlier. Clancy, according to Mitchum, had connections that were not strictly legal. 'I'm coming down the steps one night' he recalled, 'and I hear these guys talking. I look around the stairway, and I see Al Capone and another guy sitting in the living-room having a beef about "receipts". I knew enough to go back upstairs.'

With or without the benefit of these 'receipts', with or without this stepfather, the Mitchums were far from affluent, the kids sharing clothes in the time-honoured way of minimising family expenditure. But they were outgoing enough: sister Julie was already making a name for herself as a singer and dancer, while Robert, encouraged by his mother, had a poem published in the local newspaper before his age was in double figures.

10

When Anne did marry Cunningham-Morris the children gave him a rough time. He was a tremendous character, having soldier-adventured his way around the world, but he was still just a stepfather, and 'we kids didn't give this one much of a break for a long time. He had a box full of medals from World War I, photos of himself on camels in Egypt, climbing out of old biplanes in France, saluting the quarterdeck on wind-jammers in Australia. When we were very small we couldn't understand that he was full of shrapnel and couldn't work hard enough to keep us all together as a family unit. He was a very interesting man, but I couldn't see it at first.'

After the marriage Cunningham-Morris stayed on in Bridgeport, working on the newspaper, but the rest of the family moved, presumably for financial reasons, to live with Anne's parents, now settled in rural Delaware. Moving was to become a familiar experience for the kids in the next few years—they were frequently the new kids in town, 'always put in the position of proving ourselves. The trick was to push the challenger's nose to the back of his brain without giving him a cerebral haemorrhage.'

They only stayed a year or so in Delaware, exchanging the rural calm for New York's bustle when sister Julie landed a dancing job in the Big Apple. Robert went to Haaren High School on Tenth Avenue, a tough school in the middle of the notorious Hell's Kitchen district, and he quickly discovered that a tough life-style was necessary for survival. He was almost expelled for pea-shooting a teacher, but his mother intervened to suggest that a creative hobby—saxophone-playing—would straighten him out. It didn't; shortly afterwards he was expelled for dropping a firecracker into someone's horn during a school concert. According to an interview he gave in 1982 Mitchum was spending his after-school hours as a lyric arranger at WMCA. 'At the age of fifteen?' the incredulous interviewer asked. He declined to repeat himself.

This particular story also suffers from the discrepancy that at fifteen Mitchum had reputedly already left school for a life on the open road. Indeed, according to some reports, the family had returned to Delaware before he reached fourteen. Not that it greatly matters; the picture of the young Mitchum which emerges is as clear in essentials as it is dubious in detail. He was a capable young man, with a tough exterior that concealed an unusual sensitivity. The local hooligan who wrote poetry, and who was more wary of the poetry than the other hooligans. These two sides of his character would continue the fight for his soul throughout his life, but it was their very coexistence which would make him so distinguished an actor and so unusual a star.

11

At the age of fourteen (or fifteen) he quit school and took to the road. What his mother and stepfather thought of this is not known, and he himself has never given a satisfactory explanation of his departure. He says he was always in trouble, that the girls preferred his brother, but one suspects that the itch to go just coincided with an itch to be gone.

The America of 1932 which he set out to explore was hardly a traveller's paradise. The Great Depression was still deepening and the roads were full of families dispossessed by tumbling statistics on Wall Street. The young Mitchum, like everyone else, seems to have had an inner compass set for California, but he was in no hurry to get there. The world was suddenly a very big place with something very interesting around

Lone Star Trail, 1943

every corner. He 'rode underneath trains, inside the boxcars and, when I heard a guard coming, on the girders. All over!'

In 1985 it seems quite extraordinary that a fourteen-year-old kid could wander across country, never sure of where his next meal would come from or whether it would come at all. For Mitchum it had to be a formative experience, a testing of himself and his view of the world, a crucible of values and opinions. He made friends everywhere, and they weren't always the sort of friends 'society' recommended. He came into frequent contact with the 'authorities', often in circumstances calculated to foster within him a deep distrust of authority.

13

Depressions are wonderful exposers of social structure—the connections between the legal and economic systems is never clearer—and the young Mitchum's natural, adolescent anti-authoritarianism hardened into a lifetime conviction. Since, in those days, 'it was a crime to be poor', many of the 'criminals' Mitchum met up with were people just like himself, unhappily caught on the wrong side of laws framed by people with money. It didn't make him into a socialist—that was probably too authoritarian a response for a young American—but it did turn him into a lifelong anarchist, a believer in people rather than governments. The latter were just one more obstacle in a race that was already difficult enough.

He came across malnutrition and death; twice he had bouts of the food-deficiency disease, pellagra, himself. He discovered an intense claustrophobia while working as a miner in Pennsylvania. Sometimes, he admitted, 'I cried myself to sleep, wondering what my mother was thinking', but at others the mere fact of motion seemed an 'adequate philosophy'. 'Moving around like I did . . . I could be just any place, not high maybe but somehow alone and free.' The ambivalence of his existence was perfectly captured in a poem he wrote on his travels:

Trouble lies in sullen pools along the road I've taken
Sightless windows stare the empty street
No love beckons me save that which I've forsaken
The anguish of my solitude is sweet.

It was all experience, the lack of which he would later bemoan in the children and actors of a more affluent age.

Of course there were some experiences he could have done without, even if they would one day add lustre to the studio's press hand-outs. In July 1933 he arrived in Savannah, Georgia with thirty-eight dollars and an appetite. While looking for a café he was picked up by the local gendarmerie for vagrancy. 'When I told him I had thirty-eight dollars, he just called me a so-and-so wise guy and belted me with his club and ran me in.'

Five days later he appeared in court on the vagrancy charge. At least *he*'d thought it was on the vagrancy charge. 'Suddenly I realise I'm listening to a burglary case. A couple of fuzz get up and describe the burglar that hit the shoe store, and it dawns on me that they're giving an exact description of me. Then in a daze I hear the fuzz that arrested me testify that forty dollars had been heisted from the shoe store and that when they took me in I still had thirty-eight on me.'

Burglary carried a ten to twenty-year sentence in Georgia.

Mitchum, presumably heart-in-mouth, had the presence of mind to ask the judge when the burglary had taken place. Wednesday, came the judicial reply. But I was in your jail on Wednesday, Mitchum countered. The judge, shaken but not stirred by this defence, replied: 'Well, I guess I can't hold you on that charge, but a nice little indeterminate sentence for vagrancy should straighten you out.'

Actually it was a 180-day stint on the chain-gang, and not even at the county's expense. The good people of Savannah—well, some of them—were making a nice little profit out of their law and order, spending 36 cents a day on their prisoners' upkeep and receiving two dollars a day back for the work they performed on the farms of the local community-pillars. Mitchum's first night was spent sleeping on the floor next to a prisoner dying of a tubercular haemorrhage. 'They kept him alive and turned him out on the road next day so he wouldn't die inside. They didn't want the fucking book-work and all that shit. They didn't want to dig him a hole.'

Mitchum had trouble with both the authorities and some of his fellow prisoners, but he also found supporters. 'The fellows who were kind to me were the murderers, you know, the long-timers . . . they wouldn't let anyone take advantage of me.' They also helped him with his 'clothes and everything' when he made his escape, leaping for the tall timber with bullets whining around his head. The bullets missed, and 'that was that . . . in those days they wouldn't spend sixty cents to catch you if they missed you with a rifle. They'd just go out and round up somebody else to take your place.'

A few weeks later he reached home in a sorry state. The blisters and cuts left by the shackles had become badly infected, and there was talk of an amputation. His mother wouldn't hear of such a thing, deciding instead that she'd boil out the poison. Day and night for a week she applied hot poultices until at last the swelling went down, and even then Mitchum was forced to walk with crutches for some time.

It was in this garb of the wounded hero that he first met Dorothy. She was fourteen, the age, according to him, 'when a girl falls for derelicts'. Dorothy later claimed not to have liked him at first: 'he never thought of paying a compliment like the other boys. Instead, he teased. Yet every other boy I knew seemed dull by comparison.' Within a few weeks they both knew, in his words, that 'this was *it*'.

He got local work for a few months on one of the New Deal schemes, but once the family had decided to move West in the fall of 1934—to join Julie and her new husband in Long Beach—Robert and his brother decided to make their way across country at a more leisurely pace. After various adven-

tures with drunken hillbillies and railroad cops, they rejoined the rest of the family in the golden state.

Mitchum soon took off again, pulled by his wanderlust and probably pushed by a young man's need to distance himself from the family circle. In Washington state he met an Indian whom dogs found irresistible and the trade of 'dognapping' was born. 'We started taking walks around all the rich residential districts. The dogs would leave their neat little gardens and follow my partner home. We'd wait a couple of days, until the reward notices went up or were put in the local paper; then we'd return the dogs to their owners and collect the money. It was a lot of fun at the time.'

Which was more than could be said for working in a Toledo auto factory, where he spent most of the winter of 1935–6. The work was boring, and Toledo wasn't exactly the most exciting place in America. It was here, according to his probation submission in 1948, that he first tried marijuana. A friend had got him the job, but the friend's father, who owned the factory, apparently grew increasingly irritated by Mitchum's habits, notably his refusal to wear socks! Fired, Mitchum visited Dorothy and then set out once more for California, only to have his journey interrupted by a brief boxing career. He took on twenty-seven other hopefuls during the summer of 1936 in Nevada, gaining in the process more scars than money. 'I want folks to know I was licked', he insisted in later years, 'I hate fighting. It's too painful. It's not good for me. I much prefer the quiet life.'

Perhaps he was beginning to believe it even then. He'd now spent five years on the move, and five years of odd jobs and living hand-to-mouth was probably enough. And there was Dorothy, waiting patiently in Delaware, to think of. Arriving back in Long Beach in time for his nineteenth birthday, Mitchum seems to have decided that the drifting had to stop.

But what else could he do with his life? Sister Julie had one answer—join her at the Long Beach civic theatre, where she was acting, organising and generally enjoying herself. Mitchum had no great Thespian urge, but this seemed a better bet than wandering the continent. He auditioned and was accepted. Through 1936–7 he worked at the theatre, moving scenery, acting, writing. He still had no vocational feeling for the acting part, but he'd never 'had so much fun before. The theatre seemed fine to me because you could dress yourself out

Bar 20, 1943

17

of the wardrobe—so it was real easy on clothes. We used to dress up in harlequin outfits. Julie would come on with bells on her toes, and we wore long fur coats like Groucho Marx . . . I got sort of hooked on it there and then.'

The writing side he took more seriously, always had and always would. Here the ambivalence which would mark his cinematic career was already well in evidence. He had written poetry since childhood, and contemplated the cost just as long. Looking back on the publication of his poem in the local paper he noted that 'this small spotlight on our material impoverishment inspired in me an introspection ever at odds with my desire for expression'. The desire persisted, but so did the need for privacy, and poetry was too revealing. 'I think the price of poetry,' he said in 1982, 'is that it opens the door to more people that I have room for.'

Writing plays and short stories was at least one step short of poetic self-revelation, and during this period he wrote several of each. They were generally well-received, a couple winning him awards and the sort of critical acclaim which made him squirm with embarrassment. The one short story about a fashion photographer's drunken romancing in Florida was published by a literary quarterly, one play, *Fellow Traveller*, found its way mysteriously into the hands of Eugene O'Neill. He liked it enough to append notes that were longer than the play. Mitchum described the plot in 1973: 'It was about Harry Bridges being deported. He's shipped out of the country because of his union activities, and he organises the ship in transit. When there's a fire in the hold, Bridges is suspected of sabotage, so they put him ashore on a cannibal island in the South Pacific. There's nobody there but a little toothless Barry Fitzgerald Englishman who's married to a giant Negress native. Umn . . . then the next visitor is a sort of Peter Ustinov bearded member of the OGPO. Finally, there's a wedding ceremony, and Bridges is given the biggest—always the biggest—the biggest, fattest broad on the island. And he's also awarded a trophy—the shrunken head of the OGPO guy. The play winds up with a minstrel song. It was nothin' really. It was written before the war, and it did prognosticate the forthcoming Japanese situation. Those honchos at the Theatre Guild thought it was somethin' remarkable though.'

Mitchum was by 1973 quite happy to dismiss the play as 'a piece of shit' with 'one or two good sections in it'. An oratorio which he wrote, and which was directed by Orson Welles at the Hollywood Bowl in 1939, he likewise dismissed in retrospect as a 'vaudeville black-out'. But what did he feel about such achievements at the time, achievements that were really quite remarkable for someone of his age? There's no doubt that he possessed a real, if still raw, talent as a theatrical writer, and every chance to make it in the theatrical world, but he shied away from committing himself to such a direction, preferring instead to make a living writing night-club routines and risqué songs. Was it that world he shied away from, or the self-revelation implied, or the fear of losing himself? In 1972 he implied it was all three: 'I found myself either desperately inarticulate, seeking scan and rhythm, or hopelessly, esoterically over-articulate—and either way it was hopeless. I guess I thought I would become the darling of the ladies literary society and they'd pat me on the ass and endow me with profound meanings that I never really had and knew nothing about.'

Writing for the movies, which he seems to have dabbled in for a time, was no solution. He could retain his privacy, but he couldn't express himself: the studio wanted 'treatments', not writing.

Mitchum gave up trying to unite his vocation and his earning of a living. He kept writing, but for himself; the living would be earned in less revealing ways. From September 1939 to March 1940 he worked as a barker for mobile astrologist Carroll Richter. 'I'd drum up interest among the guests at the hotels, and we charged a dollar admission for people wanting to find out what was giving with the stars. After the old guy gave his spiel, I'd pitch the women into having a horoscope reading.'

This job, though 'really on vacation', offered a steady and secure income, and it must have dawned on Mitchum that he'd been keeping his sweetheart waiting long enough. He left Richter and headed north. By his own account he 'got off the Greyhound bus in Delaware in my thin ice-cream suit and Panama hat—and promptly fell on my nose in four feet of snow. Dorothy picked me up, and I told her the whole sad story, and she said, "I don't think you're fit to be let loose any longer. I suggest we get married".' On 16 March 1940 they did just that.

Back in California he resumed his freelance career writing gags and songs for night-club performers, but after a year or so he was tired of working at home and fed up with chasing creditors. In the spring of 1941 he finally decided that 'if a feller was married and there was a war on, then he got himself a lunch-box and really went to work. So I did that. I quit writing, got myself a lunch-box and went to work in the Lockheed aircraft plant.' He was there for a year, building the obsolete Lockheed-Hudsons for the desperate British with 'no faith and no enthusiasm'. His abiding memory of the place was the metal-shaping machine, which was 'something by Edgar Allan Poe out of *The Fall of the House of Usher*. It went at about

26,000 revolutions per minute and had great knives sticking out all over it . . . if one of those knives came loose, look out! One did come loose one day, made a big hole in a guy, went right on through the building and landed some place in Glendale. I was nervous as hell about that machine and I figured that whatever I chose to do in later life, I couldn't do it with a hole in me.'

At first he was on the day shift, which at least allowed him time to relax in theatrical pursuits after work, but in 1942 he was moved onto the night shift, and what with the noise generated by baby son Jim he found sleep increasingly hard to come by. Eventually his body delivered a serious warning signal to his brain—his sight gave out. On the way home from work one morning he found he couldn't read the signs on the bus-stops. 'My sight got progressively worse and when I walked up the hill to get home I found I could hardly see at all.'

Fortunately his doctor was a sensible man. He told Mitchum that the condition was simply a psychologically-induced response to his hatred of the job he was doing. He'd have to quit, there was no alternative.

While Mitchum was wondering what else he could do his mother suggested movie-acting. Well, why not? He already had the contacts; artists' manager Paul Wilkins had promised to help get such work if he ever wanted it. So the round of auditions began, with Mitchum filling in the times in between as an unsuccessful salesman in a shoe shop. Eventually he found himself at United Artists, on the other side of a desk from producer Pop Sherman, who told him not to shave or cut his hair until he was contacted. A few days later the call came. Mitchum was to report for shooting at a desert location outside Bakersfield.

Girl Rush, 1944

20

2 From Henchman to Hero

With Kim Hunter in *When Strangers Marry*, 1944

'I never will believe that there is such a thing as a great actor.'

(Mitchum, 1948)

MITCHUM ARRIVED at the location to find cast and crew sitting around looking distinctly gloomy. *Border Patrol*, the Hopalong Cassidy movie which they were supposed to be making, seemed to be going nowhere fast, and its star, looking as glum as the rest, pointed the new boy towards the make-up cabin.

There he found Earl Mosher ready with the requisite gear. 'That seems a little sticky,' Mitchum said, after examining the cowboy hat. 'No problem,' Mosher told him. 'See, the guy you're replacing, well, he was doing a stunt today, and he was pulled off his wagon, and the reins were lashed around his wrists, and, well, the wagon kept going back and forth over him, the horse went nuts, you know, when he fell, so what we got here is a little of his blood on the hat. We take care of that

Nevada, 1944

fine though.' He scraped the dried blood off with his penknife. 'There, that ought to fit just right, now.'

All of which explained the gloomy faces outside. 'I got a dead man's hat,' Mitchum pithily explained to *Rolling Stone* in 1983, 'and I've been selling horse-shit ever since.'

First, though, he had to ride the horse. It looked wild enough to have killed his predecessor, but according to Mitchum no one actually told him that it was the same horse. It threw him forty feet, just to make an equine point. 'Three times this happened, and then they gave me another horse.' He had passed his Hollywood initiation ceremony, and the cameras began rolling again on the forty-third Hopalong Cassidy movie.

It was a good introduction to the business. This most famous of all the Hollywood 'B' movie series was certainly pure formula, but it was a good formula, almost invariably well-presented and scripted. William Boyd's Hoppy was quite original as Western heroes went, unusually suspicious of violence and older/wiser than most. He always travelled with two companions, an older man to provide the humour and a young protégé to wow the female fans. The films were slow-paced for most of their length, relying on plot and character until the moment came when everybody took off in a mad chase to rescue whoever needed rescuing. In *Border Patrol* Hoppy was wearing his Texas Ranger hat, his adversary an unscrupulous mine-owner employing Mexican slave-labour to dig his silver. In *Hoppy Serves a Writ* and *The Leather Burners*, which swiftly followed, rustlers were the enemy, and in all three films Mitchum played one of the villains' henchmen, terse, bearded, and soon to discover the error of his ways. He put his casting down to 'looking a little crafty about the eyes', and was most grateful for his scruffy appearance—'all that beard muffled the dialogue'.

So, in not much more than a few weeks, he had become an experienced bit-part player. In the next year or so he was to appear in some twenty films, most of them equally undistinguished. He made another four Hoppy films—*Colt Comrades, Bar 20, False Colors* and *Riders of the Deadline*—and in the second-named was actually allowed to play one of the unshaven good guys. More modern forms of war were naturally uppermost in many people's thoughts, and Mitchum appeared in seven war movies during this year. Three of them—*Aerial Gunner, We've Never Been Licked* and *Minesweeper*—were typical B's of the era, long on action, patriotism and posthumous heroes, short on everything else. In each case he played one of the less prominent comrades-in-arms.

The other four, all major budget productions, were a more

diverse bunch. *Corvette K-225* was a Randolph Scott vehicle, based around the familiar 'new captain licks new crew into shape' formula. *Cry Havoc*, by contrast, was one of that rare breed—a woman's war movie. Six star actresses were enlisted to portray six nurses in retreat from the Japanese in the Philippines, and one of them, Ella Raines, provided the lap in which Mitchum's young soldier breathes his last. *Gung Ho* was another Universal showcase for Scott, now leading an American attack on a Japanese-occupied island. Mitchum had a dramatic scene in this one, when, wounded and laid out on a stretcher, he sees a Japanese sniper about to pot one of the doctors. Unable to shout—the bullet hole is in his throat—he heroically forces his body into a sitting posture and kills said sniper with his throwing-knife. Gung Ho indeed. *Mr Winkle Goes to War*, though just as patriotic in tone, was very different in style. Edward G. Robinson played Winkle, a bank clerk who enlists despite his advanced age and of course proves his worth. Mitchum was one of his instructors, occasionally glimpsed drifting across the back of the screen.

Between making Hoppy films and war films he appeared in two lacklustre musical comedies (*Follow the Band, Doughboys in Ireland*), a superior soap opera (*The Human Comedy*), a Laurel and Hardy (*The Dancing Masters*), and another two westerns (*The Lone Star Trail, Beyond the Last Frontier*), both as clichéd as their titles. With the exception of the last-named, in which he played a villain converted to godliness by events and his conscience, the parts were all fairly nondescript.

Nevertheless it had been a good year. He had worked for all the major studios but Warners, and he had made a lot of useful contacts. On those few occasions when he had been asked for anything more than mere competence he had duly obliged. Studio bosses looking around for new faces to fill their war-depleted rosters could hardly fail to notice him.

Mitchum was content. 'I was working in movies. I was getting a hundred bucks a week plus all the horse manure I could take home. From then on my fortune was made. I had a deep baritone voice that was hard to mix, and the only concession I ever made to movies was to lighten it. I never went after a job. They just seemed to come after me. The bread kept getting better, and it sure as hell beat punching a time clock.'

As 1944 progressed the parts started getting better too. In *Johnny Doesn't Live Here Anymore*, one of those comedies built around an apartment which, unknown to its 'users', changes hands, he had a brief but important role as a navy officer who sets things to rights. In *Thirty Seconds over Tokyo*, one of MGM's major war movies that year, he played his last minor role as a crewman on one of the planes involved in the first bombing raid on Japan. During production the director, Mervyn LeRoy, uttered his immortal judgement on Mitchum's acting ability: 'You're either the lousiest actor in the world or the best . . . I can't make up my mind which.' Mitchum has often recalled this quote, usually adding that he's never been able to decide himself.

His real breakthrough came with *When Strangers Marry*, a murder mystery in which he played the second male lead. Views of this film vary markedly, with some connoisseurs of the genre considering it mundane, while one, Don Miller, went on record as considering it the 'finest B movie ever made'. Either way Mitchum got his first personal review, *Variety* noting that he had 'a breezy quality to fit his role as the boyfriend'.

The bosses at RKO obviously had faith in him, for in June 1944 they offered him a long-term studio contract. It meant a cut in the actor's earnings and an end to any freedom of choice where projects were concerned, but it also offered a secure income, and with the deferment on his military enlistment unlikely to last much longer, a wife, two children and an extended family to support, that was what mattered. Mitchum signed on the dotted line.

His first role as a contract player was in the musical western *Girl Rush*. The director, Gordon Douglas, had been impressed by one of Mitchum's earlier performances, but he apparently had some trouble selling the actor to producer John Auer. Mitchum, waiting hopefully outside the latter's office, heard the remark 'but he looks like a monster' wafting out through the door.

He got the part anyway, playing a footloose prospector who gets caught up in a predictable story-line. *Variety* noticed him again—either his agent or the studio was working overtime—and praised his 'smooth performance' and 'likeable personality'. And better was to come. Not everyone thought he looked like a monster, and RKO decided that he would star in their new series of B westerns based on Zane Grey stories. The first one, *Nevada*, hit the screens late in 1944, and Mitchum's playing of the tough-laconic hero was a hit. 'The actor certainly justifies the faith placed in him, delivering a performance that is smack in the groove,' said the *Film Daily* reviewer. 'The fellow does himself pretty, dishing out the heroic stuff.' It must have been a nice change from gnashing his teeth at Hoppy from boot-level.

Publicity shot for *West of the Pecos*, 1945

28

A second in the series swiftly followed. Mitchum was Pecos Smith in *West of the Pecos*—the title referred to the river, not him—and once again he triumphed over evil and claimed the heroine, who he'd mistaken for a boy for most of the film. The plot featured a totally improbable series of events, the script was packed with clichés, but Mitchum's natural authority still shone through. Reviewer Kate Cameron, who had already seen a press showing of his next film, told her readers: 'Remember Mitchum's name, for you are going to hear it again and again after the release of *GI Joe*.'

Less than two years had passed since Mitchum's arrival on the set of *Border Patrol*, but this swift rise through the ranks of Hollywood's hopefuls could hardly be described as a triumph of the will. Presumably he did care, did have the ambition to transcend bit-playing, but for those around him it must have been hard to tell. Tomkies mentions that producers would ring up his agent after audition-interviews and complain about his attitude. 'He acts like he doesn't *want* to play the role,' they'd say. Mervyn LeRoy took Mitchum along to see RKO producer Frank Ross during casting for *The Robe*, and Ross, after looking Mitchum over as if he were a piece of meat, pronounced him suitably clean-cut. The actor then proceeded to devour a huge bowlful of walnuts, avocadoes and oranges which sat on the producer's table.

On another occasion Mitchum met RKO producer Sid Rogell to discuss his new contract with the company. 'We'll have to change your name, of course,' Rogell told him. 'That Mitchum tag. It's no good. We'll call you Mitchell.' 'The hell you will,' Mitchum replied. 'Now listen, guy,' Rogell insisted. 'This the way out?' Mitchum asked. He got his own way, but he might not have done. The suspicion persists that although he wanted to make his way up the Hollywood ladder, the price he was prepared to pay in terms of personal integrity was close to zero.

His landing of the role which would provide the final, crucial push into the star bracket illustrated his apparent diffidence. Of course, it all depends on which story you believe. According to Robert Aldrich, who was William Wellman's assistant director on *The Story of GI Joe*, it was he who had recommended Mitchum for the role after seeing him in the two Zane Grey westerns. According to Wellman and Mitchum—both of whom enjoyed a good story—the director was walking down the street when he saw 'this guy'. 'I asked him, "Hey, you in pictures?" "What's it to you?" "My name's Bill Wellman," I told him, "and I'm going to do Ernie Pyle's

GI Joe."' Mitchum hardly jumped at the opportunity. 'Aw, come on,' he said, 'everyone's after that role—Gary Cooper, all the rest.' It's hard to decide whether Mitchum used an apparent lack of confidence to hide a real indifference, or an apparent indifference to hide a real lack of confidence.

Wellman could hardly complain: he hadn't exactly jumped at the project himself. Pyle's novel was about the infantry, and Wellman, as he forcibly reminded producer Cowan, was 'an old broken-down flyer. I hate the goddamned infantry. I'm not interested.' But Cowan was persistent; he was convinced that this could be the definitive movie about the ordinary American foot-soldier, and he eventually wore down Wellman's resistance. Burgess Meredith was signed up to play Pyle.

Having found Mitchum on the street the director took him back to the studio for a test. This, he decided afterwards, had been his greatest mistake. Mitchum was too good. 'Burgess Meredith was there and I gave them the scene where Mitchum's character is writing letters telling mothers back home that their kids are dead. It's a beautiful scene. I did the test up against an old wagon wheel they had on one of the stages. I hated tests—and this one I should have done as a scene. Because as Mitchum played it, I suddenly heard magic, for one of the few times in my life. I was so goddamned mad at myself because I knew he could never be as great as he was in the test. He's a gutsy sonovabitch. When he realised this was his one big chance, boy, did he take it!'

The film fully deserved all the plaudits which would be heaped on it. Wellman turned the studio lot into something approaching a combat zone, with four feet of ice-cold mud topped up each night by the special effects department. Reporting to work each day the actors were loaded up with 80lb packs and ordered into the mud fully-clothed. When anyone complained Wellman would shout 'that's how real soldiers live, so get in there!'

There are two realities which *GI Joe* conveys like no other war movie—the sheer exhaustion and the unutterable mess of twentieth-century military conflict. The soldiers get in and out of trucks, wade through rivers, march through the teeming rain, sink down behind broken walls for shelter from the wind and the enemy alike. They live, and die, in the bubble of each other's company. Both their superiors and the enemy are virtually invisible. There is little actual combat in the film but this accentuates rather than diminishes the palpable, ever-present threat of sudden death. The scene which Wellman used as a test is quite astonishing, with Mitchum and Meredith lamenting the sheer waste of it all. 'If only we could create

31

something good out of all this energy,' Mitchum says.

His acting in this scene is made all the more remarkable by the hints of inexperience which come through in his playing of lesser scenes. For the first time in his career he was intensely moving; as Wellman said, he'd grabbed the chance to prove that he could express something other than cardboard heroism or cardboard villainy. A star had been born.

And, being Mitchum, he chose this moment to explode the tensions that had been building up in his personal life.

He was enlisted into the US Army one Tuesday early in 1945, having spent at least part of the previous weekend in jail. This much seems certain. But when it comes to the reason for, and the duration of, this short sojourn behind bars, facts seem harder to come by.

In his probation plea written four years later Mitchum recounted the incident in question, in the process raising more questions than he answered. 'Five days prior to my induction,' he wrote, 'I was jailed. Out to obtain a prescription for a sick child, I called my wife to discuss the prescription, and my sister answered the phone. She refused to allow me to talk to my wife and hung up the receiver. There followed several attempts, all of which had the same results, until finally, knowing my sister to be hostile to my wife (who was also ill and bedded), I told her that I would come to talk to Dorothy and demand an accounting before her. Upon arrival I was met by two sheriff's deputies and arrested. Pressed for complaint, my sister refused to sign, and at my own demand for justice, I was arrested, roundly beaten and booked at the Fairfax Avenue sheriff's station.'

Why, one wonders, was his sister at his house, if she and his wife were hostile to each other? Why was he demanding an accounting from his wife? If this was all part of some marital row, why was his sister protecting his wife, whom she apparently had no time for? Who called the police?

A very different version of events was offered by Mitchum in 1983. His absence from home is not mentioned, the prescription is not mentioned, his wife and sister are not mentioned. Mitchum was just sitting on his porch enjoying a drink and a cigarette when a man rushed up the steps shining a light into his face. Mitchum knocked him back down the steps, breaking his nose. The man turned out to be a cop at the wrong address. Did Mitchum apologise for hitting him? Like hell he did. 'If the cops are going to come and hassle you, then I wanted them to take it all the way. I mean, what the hell? Let's go through with it. Right?'

So he leapt into the cop car shouting, 'Let's go downtown right now, motherfuckers!' The cops were also getting into the spirit of the thing. With fists, billy-clubs and gun-butts they set to work on the indignant Mitchum, breaking two of his ribs. Then they took him downtown.

According to the probation plea, 'the next morning I was advised by the captain of detectives to plead guilty to a charge of being in an "intoxicated condition on private property" (over my objections) and pay a $10 fine and "forget about it". This I did and was sentenced by the late Cecil Holland to a term in the county jail, admitted Saturday, discharged on Sunday.'

According to the 1983 *Rolling Stone* interview he was offered the guilt-plea advice by his lawyer, but the judge refused to play ball, giving him a six month sentence instead of the expected $10 fine. Mitchum protested on the grounds that he was going into the Army, and the judge relented. He had the cops take Mitchum to the enlistment centre, then bring him back to jail for several days, and finally deliver him, on the Tuesday, to the troop train.

Neither of these versions of the events offers a picture of a contented family man on the verge of a brilliant career in the movies. The first version suggests a far-from-happy family situation, the second a man living at the extremity of his nerves. Enlistment into the Army saved Mitchum this time; three years later there would be no such surrogate jail on offer.

His military experience was not exhilarating. He never left America, spending the whole eight months at Fort MacArthur as a drill instructor and medical assistant. The latter job required RKO's new star to look up 'the asshole of every GI in America', in search of 'piles, haemorrhoids, bananas, grapes, dope . . . you name it'. He met 'the same type of guys I used to bum around with', and they spent most of their time 'swapping lies'. When it was time for him to be discharged the authorities decided that 'it would be bad reflection on the army if I came out a private. So some officers marked one chevron on my sleeve and I came out a PFC.'

As a screen soldier he had proved rather more successful, as he discovered on re-entering civilian America. *Newsweek* noted his 'fine performance' in *GI Joe*, while Kate Cameron in the *Daily News* thought it 'the best performance of the year', the source of the film's 'power and glory'. General Eisenhower weighed in with the opinion that it was the greatest war pic-

Overleaf: The Story of GI Joe, 1945

ture he'd ever seen. James Agee was more specific: 'Coming as it does out of a world in which even the best work is nearly always compromised, and into a world which is generally assumed to dread honesty and courage and to despise artistic integrity, it is an act of heroism, and I cannot suggest my regard for it without using such words as veneration and love . . . it seems to me a tragic and eternal work of art.'

For his part, Mitchum was nominated for an Academy Award in the Best Supporting Actor category. He didn't win, but he must nevertheless have been proud of both the performance and the film.

GI Joe had been made by United Artists, with Mitchum on loan from RKO, and he must have wondered how many chances he'd get to display his talent with the company he'd signed for, a company not always noted for tackling serious subjects in a serious manner.

RKO had seen some dramatic ups and downs over the previous seven years. In 1938 it had been close to bankruptcy, and the new President, George Schaeffer, had sought financial viability by moving the product up-market. B movies, the company's traditional stock-in-trade, had still been churned out, but they had been joined by a host of prestige A productions. At first this mix had proved successful—the receivers had been seen off.

Then along came Orson Welles. *Citizen Kane* and *The Magnificent Ambersons*, though both classic movies by any standard, destroyed Schaeffer's financial recovery. Both flopped at the box office, and *Citizen Kane* sucked RKO into a long and extremely costly legal wrangle with newspaper tycoon Randolph Hearst, who had taken great exception to Welles' alleged portrayal of his life. The actor/director seemed blithely unconcerned by all this, and by 1942 was busy making *It's All True* with scant regard for budgetary restraint. Schaeffer resigned, Charles Koerner took over.

'All's well that ends Welles' was the new management catchphrase. Koerner pulled the plug on *It's All True*, and took the company a notch back down-market with a more balanced mix of popular movies. Potboilers, war films, westerns, musicals, comedies, horror films—all would pull their weight under the new regime. And it worked; by the end of 1942, with the aid of some astute borrowing, RKO was back on an even, if somewhat precarious, keel.

1943 was even better, and in 1944 and 1945 the profitability was sustained sufficiently for Koerner to indulge in a few quality productions. As a result 1946 would be the company's most profitable year since the thirties, with films like *Notorious*, *The Spiral Staircase* and *The Best Years of Our Lives* pleasing critics and paying public alike.

Koerner died in February 1946, and the new production chief, Dore Schary, inherited this apparently healthy situation. He announced no immediate change in policy, but was well-known for believing that films should deal with important social issues, without of course sacrificing their 'entertainment value'. On the surface then, it seemed that Mitchum could hardly have picked a better company on which to tie his star. It looked like there would be big pictures and important pictures, big money and interesting parts to play.

Companies might change some policies, but the eternal truths of star-promotion remained. Mitchum, as one of RKO's blue-eyed assets, was given the treatment like any other, wheeled out in front of Hollywood's tame interviewers for the edification of the great movie-going multitude. The picture that emerged of him might bear no relation to the real person, but that seemed to bother no one, except perhaps Mitchum himself.

An article on the new star in *Picturegoer* early in 1947 was fairly typical. The actor's past was presented as an exciting preparation for his current, much beloved career, and just in case criss-crossing the country as a hobo failed to stimulate the public imagination they had him working as an engine-wiper on a boat from California to South America. No other source for this story appears to exist, and it seems quite feasible that some mini-mogul had decided that Hollywood's new emphasis on Latin America—the European market was, at this time, contracting financially as far as Hollywood was concerned—should be reflected in the stars' biographies. Mitchum's late enlistment into the Army was not, of course, his fault, but having a family to support was not considered an exciting enough reason. He had tried to enlist, the article claimed, but had been rejected because of injuries received in a fight. This didn't square too well with the actor's later statement: 'When they took me away, I still had bits of the porch rails under my fingernails.'

No matter. The new star was adventurous, patriotic and a bit wild. Now to the serious stuff. 'Robert is six feet one inch in height, and has hazel eyes and light brown hair. He is one of the most unaffected persons in pictures, and is never happier than when he is at home. He thinks that getting into pictures was just good luck and not due to any particular talent on his part. His ambition is merely to make a good living and he sincerely hopes that he will never "go Hollywood". He likes people, is a great kidder, has no pretence, has no desire to own a ranch, and never rides a horse except for pictures. He is completely natural when at work before the cameras, never using any make-up. Robert Mitchum—that is his real name, by the way—spends all his spare time with his wife and two children. They live in a rented house in West Hollywood, and, despite the fact that home means so much to him, Robert never has any wish to work around a house or garden.'

Well, this guy's almost perfect. Successful but humble. Sincere but fun. Rebellious, but not so as his family would notice. He doesn't even hunger for a ranch.

But, apparently this wasn't good enough. Another article in *Picturegoer* two years later tried to fill in some imaginary gaps. He had now been born of 'theatrical stock', and had turned down 'a tentative offer of a part on Broadway' before engine-wiping his way to South America. Back home from riding the banana boat he had, on family advice, 'enrolled at Duke University' and 'by an effort endured two years of academic study'. However he was still 'without any ambition to own a ranch'.

The columnists' inventive approach to historical research hardly creates much confidence in the contemporary powers of observation, but Sidney Skolsky did offer a picture of Mitchum around this time which sounds authentic enough. 'He is in awe of no one,' Skolsky wrote, 'and still fools around with the pals he had before fame. He will often startle or amuse his leading lady. He is famed among friends for his impersonations. He is a good mimic and does, among others, Katharine Hepburn and Charles Laughton well. He has fooled Ronald Coleman with his English accent. He is a good baritone . . . He seldom gets angry and gets along well with everyone. He has no peeves or superstitions but still occasionally knocks on wood. He drops clothes on the floor while undressing, sports tweeds, knitted ties and long pointed collars. He has a large lunch and a huge dinner. His favourites are porterhouse steak and red wine. He dislikes fancy dressers. He can and does cook when necessary. He smokes any available, having no favourite brand. He even rolls his own expertly when he has to. Anyone he can't remember he calls Peter and that goes for females too . . .'

When it came to analysing the reasons for his success as an actor the columnists were somewhat at a loss. Marjorie Wil-

The Story of GI Joe, 1945

liams cheerfully decided that 'the personality counts more than the player'. 'Indeed,' she added wistfully, 'some among his admirers claim that he can't act for apples.' His portrayal in *GI Joe* she thought, 'owed more to Robert Mitchum the man, and to his experience of Service life than to the intuitive actor in him'. Exactly how Mitchum had interiorised the Battle of Cassino whilst inspecting posteriors at Fort MacArthur she declined to explain.

Alan Warwick was equally at a loss, suggesting to his readers that 'if you can tell me what it is about Bob Mitchum that makes him what he is, maybe you'd better write the article instead of me'. Still, he did mention the actor's 'way of making the parts he plays seem like life', and his 'streamlining'. And a thousand words or so later, having recorded the testimony of American girlhood—'we like him because he has the most immoral face we ever saw'—and his own physical inventory ('dreamy eyes . . . interesting mouth . . . enviably broad shoulders'), Warwick decides that what's special about Mitchum is that he doesn't try to impress. He's a 'natural actor without mannerisms. Look at any of his film characterisations—it's that naturalness that registers every time.' Streamlined, of course.

What did Mitchum feel about this rewriting of his past and polishing of his image? How did it gell with the praise lavished on him for his acting in the 'tragic and eternal' *GI Joe*? Didn't he feel stifled by the hyperbole, feel the urge to fight back?

Everything in his past suggests that he did, and there are some contemporary indications of his hatred for all the phoniness. He turned up at one promotion party bare-chested, didn't turn up at the Oscar ceremony at all. He sent up the columnists, or at least tried to, by telling them that he once dug a hole in his garden, and that it was still there. He needn't have bothered; they decided it was a cute joke, and never tired of repeating it.

For the most part, though, he seems to have chosen passive resistance, and over the years this would most often take the form of counterpointing 'their' hyperbole with liberal doses of self-deprecation. Looking back on this period he would claim that his ascent to the rank of 'leading man' was 'a cause for apprehension and embarrassment. It was much too late to start pursuing any particular design or direction. I knew I'd be a leading man until the string ran out.' As for *GI Joe*, it was just luck. 'No one could have missed in such a role. Coming down off a mountain strapped to a mule and having a camera panned right on my kisser . . . I was bound to click. But that doesn't mean I did any acting.'

It had nothing to do with acting ability. 'I came at a very

fortunate time,' he said in 1973, 'they wanted ordinary guys who looked ugly and there I was, all broken up. Anybody could identify with me, because I looked even worse than anyone else. It made the whole American Army feel good. I guess that was an indirect reason for us winning the war.'

He had no illusions about his place in RKO's scheme of things. 'They were looking for a journeyman actor and like everyone else had a lot of attractive people on their books. But these actors didn't have, I suppose, enough versatility. They felt I could do a number of things, so by hiring me they'd be getting a lot for the same money. I was a sort of utility man there for ten years . . . I kept telling them I couldn't ride a horse or anything. But they went all through the Hopalong Cassidy movies, then dressed everyone else up very badly and marched me out before the cameras in a tailor-made outfit. After that I was sort of on the hook. RKO opened the door for me—and I became their workhorse. Everyone had them. Twentieth Century-Fox had their workhorses. MGM had theirs. I was the workhorse of RKO. If I wanted the joint painted purple they'd paint it purple . . . I was teacher's pet.'

Mitchum's analysis of his own success, all from the vantage point of later years, seems curiously like a mirror image of the studio/columnist version. For them his star status was pre-ordained, for him it was pure fluke. Their pin-up was his ugly duckling, their dreamy-eyed Adonis was his workhorse.

Of course he didn't believe his own version anymore than he believed theirs. Exactly what he did think and feel about the process whereby Hollywood and the public sequestered a large chunk of his life will probably never be known. But it must have been hard for someone like Mitchum to live with. Some 'stars' seem to take it all in their stride, either to embrace or distance themselves from all the ballyhoo, but he seems to have internalised the conflict, with one half of himself laughing it all off with cynical one-liners, the other half secretly ashamed of his involvement in a profession which, according to Dorothy, he continued to consider in some way unmanly. This conflict would not lose its sharpness for many years, and over the next decade evidence of its continued vitality would occasionally erupt into the headlines. In the meantime Mitchum made movies.

3 The Gullible Galahad

With Jean Porter and Guy Madison in *Till the End of Time*, 1946

'I'd close my eyes and when I opened them again there was a new leading lady.'

(Mitchum, 1953)

MITCHUM'S FIRST post-discharge film was *Till the End of Time*, which, suitably enough, explored the problems confronting discharged soldiers. The people behind the camera were a prestigious bunch—Schary was producing, Edward Dmytryk directing, Niven Busch had written the original novel—and a hard-hitting film seemed in prospect.

It didn't materialise, despite convincing performances from the three male leads, all of them relative newcomers. Guy Madison, Bill Williams and Mitchum each portrayed an ex-serviceman trying to cope with the readjustment to civilian life. Each, in true Hollywood style, has a particular problem: Madison's soldier is insecure and can't re-establish contact

Off the set during the making of *Undercurrent*, 1946

45

with his parents, Mitchum's is an ex-cowboy with a steel plate in his head which drives him to drink, and Williams' is an ex-boxer now with artificial legs. They meet a girl, and predictably she chooses to sort out Madison.

Schary's influence is only really obvious in the scene featuring a confrontation between the threesome and a group of Klan-like racists, but the forcefulness of this encounter is not repeated elsewhere in the film, which meanders on, knee-deep in bad dialogue and half-submerged by an appalling Chopinesque score. The reviews were sympathetic but not enthusiastic.

Mitchum was then loaned out to MGM for *Undercurrent*, in which he played third lead behind Robert Taylor in his first post-service role and the indestructible Katharine Hepburn. He would later contemptuously refer to the film as 'Under-drawers', but it hardly merited such an exciting title. Taylor and Hepburn played a newly married couple, with wife unaware that husband is not what he seems. Mitchum, as the latter's mysterious brother, finally saves her from a premature grave.

Hepburn seems to have appreciated just how bad the film was, and chosen to take her frustration out on the young Mitchum. 'You know you can't act,' she told him, 'and if you hadn't been good-looking you would never have gotten the picture. I'm tired of playing with people who have nothing to offer.' Mitchum apparently burst out laughing, and for years afterwards would give her comment a prominent place in his self-depreciation campaign.

While shooting *Undercurrent* in the mornings, he was working on *Desire Me* in the afternoons and *The Locket* by night. The last-named was more than a cut above his two previous efforts, and has been unjustly ignored by most film historians. It is fascinating in two respects, as a movie very much of its time—its two main themes being the dangerous woman and psychiatry—and as a definite contender for the film which carried the use of flashback to its furthest extent. *The Locket* is like a Russian matryoshka doll: the scene in which the central character reveals her childhood trauma is a flashback within a flashback within a flashback.

The story begins with Nancy (Laraine Day) a few hours away from marriage to John (Gene Raymond). In that time he receives a visit from her first husband (Brian Aherne), who takes us into the first flashback. He also received a visit on the eve of his wedding to Nancy, from her ex-lover Norman (Mitchum), who told him that Nancy had already committed murder and involved him in covering it up. The first husband-to-be didn't believe Norman, who then committed suicide. Nancy's compulsive thievery, which led to the murder, is apparently the consequence of her being wrongfully accused of stealing when a child.

The fact that her obsessive behaviour seems out of all proportion to the event that triggered it has led Julian Petley to argue that a more rigorously Freudian explanation is being deliberately hinted at. He quotes Freud's remark—'the female genitals are symbolically represented by all such objects as share their characteristic of enclosing a hollow space which can take something into it'—and suggests that the locket which the child-Nancy was accused of stealing seems to fit the symbolic bill. This may be so; certainly the censors at this time would not have countenanced anything more blatant.

Lockets apart, Nancy was clearly an unconscious creation of her creator's times, the film one more in a long string of forties offerings which featured scheming *femmes fatales* leading heroes to their doom. In one way *The Locket* took this trend to its furthest extreme: of all the forties *femmes fatales* Nancy seems the most innocent, the most normal.

This rash of predatory females was no accident. During the war years women had been taken down from their pedestals and put to work for the 'common good', but once the war was over the male world didn't know quite what to do with them. The short-term answer was to knock this newly independent woman, morally-speaking, into the gutter. If the real threat to male stability and confidence couldn't be expressed, then women would be created who expressed the threat in a way which Hollywood's public recognised. Such women offered a double solace, both explaining male insecurity and providing men with a positive role in the woman's rehabilitation as a dependant. In a number of his movies during this period Mitchum played the male side of the equation, the man who got led astray, and to some extent the very creation of this character contributed to his rising popularity. Mitchum looked like he could be led astray. He looked like a man who would take risks, who would damn the moral consequences, and who would lack the energy to save himself once enmeshed in the *femme fatale*'s seductive grasp.

The Locket, for all its enduring interest, didn't fare too well with the contemporary critics, whereas *Crossfire*, which hasn't worn nearly as well, was lavished with praise. The story centred around anti-Semitism in the US Army—the orginal novel had dealt with prejudice against homosexuals—and the film's eventual producer/director team, Adrian Scott and Edward Dmytryk, had been pushing the project for some time. Koerner had refused to give the go-ahead, but Schary proved more amenable, despite continued opposition from inside the RKO boardroom. He knew something about anti-Semitism. 'During the war,' he wrote in his autobiography, 'I had gone into army camps and lectured on the causes of anti-Semitism and had seen and heard the virulent bigotry in army ranks . . . for years I had worked in the fetid field of combatting anti-Semitism and I knew something about the steamy current of hatred.' He put his foot down.

Meanwhile, Twentieth Century-Fox were planning an opus covering much the same territory. Zanuck phoned Schary to express his annoyance at the competition from RKO. Schary was 'compelled to tell him that he had not discovered anti-Semitism and that it would take far more than two pictures to eradicate it'.

Good intentions do not, unfortunately, a good film make. Scott and Dmytryk seem to have fallen into the familiar Hollywood trap of trying to use a formula genre for ideological purposes. As usual what came across was the ideology of the formula. *Crossfire* ended up a *film noir*, bearing all the emotional resonance of that fatalistic genre. The action, nearly all of which takes place at night, moves from squalid rooming houses through unkempt apartments to dimly-lit bars with all the crusading zeal of a depressed Cassandra. The anti-Semitic killer, though admirably played by the young Robert Ryan, is clearly a killer first and an anti-Semite second, which considerably dilutes the film's intended message. The insertion of a lengthy racist spiel is no substitute for genuine character motivation.

Despite this the film was a smash hit, accounting for about a quarter of RKO's profit that year. It garnered five Oscar nominations, but largely thanks to a right-wing telephone campaign—the shadow of McCarthyism was descending on Hollywood—received no awards.

Desire Me didn't get any either, though perhaps a mention as the worst film of 1947 would have been fitting. Mitchum was again out on loan to MGM, and again playing the second male in a love triangle. The story of a woman who believes her husband dead and takes in his friend, only to discover that friend has deliberately (and mistakenly) left husband for dead, might have made sense when it was first filmed in 1928 as *The Homecoming*, but somewhere along the line its credibility had all seeped away. Not surprisingly the film ends with Greer Garson consulting a psychiatrist.

The making of the film was much more interesting than the final product. Shooting commenced with Robert Montgomery

With Laraine Day and Ricardo Cortez in *The Locket*, 1946

48

in the leading role, George Cukor directing, and *A Woman of His Own* as the title. Cukor thought the script 'didn't really make any sense', and it must have showed, because after completing *a* movie he was replaced by Jack Conway. He was soon replaced by Mervyn LeRoy. Meanwhile Robert Montgomery had given way to Richard Hart and the original title to *Sacred and Profane*. LeRoy must have known what he was in for, because he arranged beforehand that his name would not appear on the credits. When Cukor saw the final version he had his name removed as well, providing the movie with its sole distinction—no directorial credit. Mitchum should have been so lucky. The *New York Herald Tribune* thought he gave 'a lot of melodramatic impact to the fight scene', but added that 'he might as well have kept his name off the credits too, so far as this film will advance his career'.

In fact, none of the first five post-war movies had done much for Mitchum's niche in cinematic history. His part in *Till the End of Time* had been a good one, and he'd received favourable personal notices, but the film itself had been nothing special. In *Undercurrent* he had been woefully miscast; years later director Vincent Minnelli revealed that Mitchum was 'never comfortable in the role of the sensitive Michael'. Much the same could be said of his part in *The Locket*. Although he was convincing enough as an insecure, jealous lover, the portrayal of a committed artist seemed beyond his range.

His role in *Crossfire* didn't come up to his expectations. He had been told it was a great part, he told Ruth Waterbury soon afterwards, but soon realised that anyone competent could have played it. 'Why did you lie to me?' he asked the producer. 'I needed your name on the marquee,' he was told.

And in *Desire Me* he had been both miscast and under-used. He appeared only at the beginning and end of the film, and had nothing much more to do than make the odd Gallic gesture and throw his rival off a cliff. At this point in time there seemed no consistent theme to his films or performances, they weren't *his* in any real sense. 'Robert Mitchum' might be up on the marquee, but as yet he had not developed a cinematic identity to put behind the name. Fortunately the next two films would go a long way towards developing one.

Pursued begins with Thorley (Teresa Wright) arriving at a ruined house perched high above Monument Valley. Jeb (Mitchum), her foster-brother and husband, is already there, waiting for his enemies and remembering a night in the same house many years before . . .

Most of the rest of the film is an extended flashback which brings the story from then to now. The child Jeb's parents have been killed, and he's being brought up by the sister of their killer, Grant, along with her own two children, Thorley and Adam. The two boys never come to terms with each other, and Grant is still around, determined to finish off the last member of the family he hates. Jeb knows nothing of his past, and his foster mother refuses to tell him the connection between the families.

One of the two boys has to enlist for the Spanish-American War, and Jeb loses the toss of a coin, but before he leaves he realises he loves Thorley. Returning a hero he revives both the love affair with her and the feud with Adam. The latter tries to bushwhack him, and Jeb shoots him dead before knowing who the assailant is. Thorley now refuses to have anything to do with him, and Grant makes the most of their estrangement. Then Thorley conceives the idea of shooting Jeb dead on their wedding-night—the ultimate punishment. But he guesses her plan, empties her gun, and after she's clicked it at him a couple of times the twosome surrender to their mutual passion. Unfortunately, Grant and cronies are gathering outside, and Jeb is forced to flee, back to the ruined house where the film began. And at last he remembers enough to piece together the dark secret which has poisoned the life of two families.

Pursued is a western, but only because that's where it takes place. In many ways it resembles *The Locket*, with the traumatic event of childhood slowly unravelled through a succession of deaths. A psychological thriller-western then, the first of its kind.

And like any psychological thriller worthy of its genre, it is atmosphere rather than plot which dominates the proceedings. Monument Valley has never looked more alien, more contemptuous of the mere humans who ride through it. The musical score is continually unsettling. The plot, though often incomprehensible on logical grounds, is clearly playing notes on a Freudian instrument. Something is happening here that Gary Cooper would never understand; the final denouement is all about sexual guilt.

Mitchum, as the man 'pursued' by a past he can't quite remember, gives a memorable performance in the fatalistic vein he was largely to make his own. Crippled by self-doubt, he nevertheless pushes himself doggedly onwards towards an explanation which he knows may destroy all his self-belief. The director, Raoul Walsh, remembered both this performance and the film with pride. Mitchum, he thought, was 'one of the finest natural actors I ever met'; the film itself had 'a quite fantastic atmosphere . . . it was almost a ghost story.'

51

Pursued could well have been called *Out of the Past*, but that title was reserved for Mitchum's next project, a classic *film noir* of the private eye variety. Again his character would spend much of the movie in flashback, recounting a past that wouldn't go away, and again he would doggedly seek a way out of its grip, this time with less success.

This was not one of Schary's movies—it had been bought before his assumption of the reins at RKO—and according to writer Daniel Mainwaring the producer was never very enthusiastic about it. This probably helped Mitchum. The film's supporters wanted Bogart for the leading role, but the lack of interest at the top forced them into using an RKO contract star.

The script was the work of more than one man. As Mainwaring explained it, he wrote the first draft from his novel *Build My Gallows High* (the film's UK title), but producer Warren Duff 'wasn't sure about it . . . when I finished and went on to something else, Duff put Jim [James M.] Cain on it. Jim Cain threw my script away and wrote a completely new one. They paid him twenty to thirty thousand and it had nothing to do with the novel or anything. He took it out of the country and set the whole thing in the city. Duff didn't like it and called me back . . . I made changes and did the final. But that's the way things used to work. You'd turn around and spit and some other writer would be on your project.'

When questioned about the family likeness shared by *Out of the Past* and *The Maltese Falcon*, Mainwaring cheerfully replied, 'well, don't think I haven't swiped from *The Maltese Falcon* often', but far from being a pale imitation, *Out of the Past* is in most respects a better film. They share the forties emphasis on the diabolic woman, and the traditional *film noir* conclusion that justice cannot be done; in both movies the private eye and the villain end up agreeing that they need a 'fall guy', because telling the truth is no longer a feasible option. They also share plots which are about as easy to disentangle as Marx Brothers' logic. But *Out of the Past*, unlike *The Maltese Falcon*, is not studio-bound, gaining an extra thematic, as well as pictorial, dimension from its juxtaposing of urban and rural settings.

It opens with a man driving into a small north Californian town. He's looking for Jeff Bailey, the local garage owner, because one of Bailey's former employers, a man named Witt, is eager to renew their acquaintance. Bailey (Mitchum) agrees,

With Laraine Day in *The Locket*, 1946

and *en route* to Witt's palatial residence he tells his current girl-friend (Virginia Huston) what it's all about . . .

At some indeterminate point in the past, while working as a private eye, he is hired by Witt (Kirk Douglas) to find and bring back the latter's girlfriend Kathi (Jane Greer), who has absconded with $40,000. He tracks her down in Acapulco and there falls victim to her spell. When she tells him that she never took the money, sweetly asking, 'Don't you believe me?', he replies 'Baby, I don't care', sealing his eventual fate. They're tracked down by Bailey's former partner, who tries blackmail and is cold-bloodedly shot by Kathi for his pains. She then vanishes, back to Witt as it later transpires, and Bailey is left with a murder charge around his neck. He hides out in the country as a garage-owner, and we're back in the present.

Witt tells him all is forgiven, but asks Bailey to do a job for him in San Francisco as a token of their mutual good will. This is another frame of course, and though Bailey is quick enough to see it he's not quick enough to avoid it. His last hope of salvation now lies in a deal with Witt, but he arrives at the palatial residence to find that Kathi's killed him as well. All is lost.

This brief plot synopsis gives him some idea of the movie's tone, the sense of helpless entrapment by fate which runs through all the labyrinthine double-crosses. Every move Bailey makes to free himself from the noose only tightens it further around his neck. Unlike Sam Spade in *The Maltese Falcon* he goes down with the heroine.

As mentioned, the way the action moves to and fro between the rural and urban worlds provides *Out of the Past* with an extra level. Outdoors there is a normally neutral nature, Virginia Huston's fresh-faced girlfriend, and Bailey largely in control of events. In the city there is darkness, Greer's (and Rhonda Fleming's) corrupt beauty, and Bailey floundering around like a fish out of water. When the hood sent by Greer to kill Bailey in the country, *his* domain, is thrown off the rocks by an expertly-cast fishing-rod line, it makes perfect sense. But every time he leaves this domain his chances diminish alarmingly.

The dialogue is excellent throughout, and the cast do it proud. Kirk Douglas, in only his second film, oozes suave malevolence without sinking into stereotype, and the 22-year-old Greer is completely believable as the amoral siren. Mitchum fits the role of Bailey like the proverbial glove, and the reviewers of the time recognised as much. The *New York Herald Tribune* pronounced him 'ideally suited to his role . . . he can fling a line of dialogue to an arrogant gunman or brush off an unwanted dame with the best of them, and he gives the 2D melodrama exactly what it requires—personality rather than character.' Bosley Crowther, reviewing for the *New York Times* found Mitchum 'magnificently cheeky and self-assured as the tangled private eye', and *Newsweek* thought him 'particularly effective as the cryptic, casual sleuth who mixes pleasure and isn't afraid to pay for it'.

Perhaps that's how it looked in 1947. What seems striking now is the extent to which Bailey, unlike the other forties private eyes, *is* afraid to pay for it. But he does it anyway. With Bogart, in either *The Maltese Falcon* or *The Big Sleep*, there's always the sense that one part of him is holding back, calculating the odds. There's a certainty tucked away somewhere which he can always cling to as a last resort. With Mitchum, in either *Out of the Past* or *Pursued*, you never get that feeling. Mitchum, like the rest of us, like real people, is quite capable of making a definitive ass of himself. He's vulnerable in a way that Bogart never is. He's also—three strikingly human characteristics—lazy, careless, and inclined to overestimate his control over events. Put him up against someone like Kathi and he's doomed. Even when joined by someone who really loves him, like Thorley, he only manages to survive through the intervention of others.

It was this vulnerability which made Mitchum so distinctive, and so useful to have around when the *femmes fatales* were stalking the celluloid jungle. Of course he was handsome, he looked and acted tough, he sounded right swapping wisecracks, but when it came to sex and romance he was downright gullible. If Mitchum came through a story the right side up there was a real sense that he'd achieved something; when most other Hollywood stars managed as much it all seemed a little too easy.

The next three films were considerably less distinguished. *Rachel and the Stranger* found Mitchum in a virtual supporting role, with William Holden's widowed farmer and Loretta Young's 'bondwoman' taking up most of the screentime. The story is set in the early nineteenth century, and the plot could be written out on a restaurant napkin. It probably was. Farmer's wife dies, farmer falls to pieces, son and friend (Mitchum) coax him back to life. He decides boy needs a mother, so he buys one and then ignores her. Friend doesn't so he gets jealous. Indians attack, are beaten off, friend departs, leaving behind newly happy couple. Sobbing in the back stalls.

Mitchum makes his entrance leading a horse, playing a

guitar and singing. He seems to be wearing designer buck-skins. He soon leaves again—it is not what anyone would consider a taxing part. He plays the frontier spirit—anti-schooling, pro-wandering, etc.—while everyone else is pro-civilisation, and in this sense the role reinforced his growing identity with a gentle form of anti-authoritarian anarchism. He's not destructive, he just wants to go his own way. As there's no Jane Greer around to lead him astray he's still singing when he departs.

Blood on the Moon was an altogether heavier affair, a range war western directed by Robert Wise. It was Wise's first big solo project and the experience gained from working on *Citizen Kane* and *The Magnificent Ambersons* with Welles was clearly evident in the film's overall mood. The interior lighting is particularly effective.

The plot is pretty routine, with Mitchum as the loner who butts into said range war, first on the side of Robert Preston's grinning villain, then to the rescue of Barbara Bel Geddes' rancher's daughter. The fist-fight scene is justly famous, and Wise remembered it with some pride. 'We tried to do something for the first time in a western: a bar-room fight that was at least realistic. We said, let's have these men go at it all the way, hard as they can, and let's have them exhausted at the end, which they would be. And I think it worked. Mitchum and Preston liked the idea very much, and I think it's the most distinctive scene in the picture.'

In a recent review of the film in *Monthly Film Bulletin* Richard Combs observes that 'Mitchum plays the outsider who drifts into the conflict between ranchers and farmers with exemplary detachment, faultlessly helpful when called upon but consistently unimpressed—by himself or anyone else.' Either the role had been tailor-made for him or he had made it his own, for it fitted perfectly around his emerging cinematic persona. Here is a man who is drawn into things by a combination of chance, curiosity, generosity and women, not by the strength of his beliefs. He carries no moral baggage, doing whatever he does because it feels right, not because he thinks it is right. He doesn't have a trace of the self-righteous hero in him.

Blood on the Moon, though not a great western, is certainly an interesting one. The only people likely to have been interested in *The Red Pony* were kids and those adults doing research into the processes whereby Hollywood mangled

With Teresa Wright in *Pursued*, 1947

decent literature. The moguls had already been persuaded by previous financial failure that straight Steinbeck was not popular on the screen, and Republic's answer to the cinematisation of *The Red Pony*, a moving and adult story, was to make a children's picture. Their borrowing of Mitchum from RKO for this, his first colour feature, marked the limit of the studio's ingenuity. That, and changing the ending to a happy one.

While these three films were being made in 1947–8 Mitchum's popularity was reaching new heights. In June 1948 *Picturegoer* breathlessly reported that in the previous October 'his mail at RKO studios amounted to over 1,600 letters, second in number to Ginger Rogers'. There was no doubting that he was now a bona fide Hollywood star.

The perks were considerable, something close to a quarter of a million dollars a year, and he seems to have had a lot of fun earning it. He called Greer Garson 'Red', which either enchanted or enraged her, depending on whose version of the story you choose to believe. He found director Raoul Walsh 'a marvellous man, he'd cry at card tricks'. Walsh would call 'Action!' and then 'turn his back on the scene and try, unsuccessfully, to roll cigarettes with one hand on the side of his bad eye. He'd fail four times or so, then he'd turn back to the actors in disgust and scream "Cut!"' The movies didn't suffer. 'The thing was, he trusted us. He wouldn't have made the picture at all, if he didn't.'

Mitchum met his match in Loretta Young, who brought her swear-box onto the set of *Rachel and the Stranger*. 'Some charity for unwed mothers,' Mitchum told Roderick Mann in 1976. 'A "damn" cost you five cents; "hell" ten; "Goddamn" twenty-five. "Listen," I told her, "What if I say – you?" "Oh," she said, "that's free".'

Ruth Waterbury had another story of this happy twosome back in 1948. They were doing a romantic scene, the lighting was doing more for her than him, and she acknowledged as much. 'Honey, I don't give a damn,' he said. The director asked for a second take, and 'Loretta moves that same infinitesimal degree again and the light is even better for her lovely face and Mitchum is more shadowed than before. But her eyes are wide when the scene is finished. "Why, you really don't give a damn, do you?" she says.' Mitchum presumably pointed out that she owed the box five cents.

With Teresa Wright in *Pursued*, 1947

58

When considering the quality of the films he was currently involved in, Mitchum must have experienced the odd doubt. In the ensuing decades he would go to great lengths to disassociate himself from the quality of the finished product, preferring to present himself as no more than a highly-paid extra. The mask did slip once in a while—in 1974 he admitted that, after entering movies for the fun and the money, he had 'started to care'. Back in 1948 he was obviously still in this 'caring stage', telling Ruth Waterbury that the dialogue in most of his films was 'so bad you have to spit it out like dirt in your teeth'. At that time he was 'not yet' in a position to do much about it, but he clearly harboured such hopes for the future.

Away from the set stardom's perks were balanced by its drawbacks. Press conferences belonged to the latter category: 'They scare hell out of me,' he admitted. 'What am I supposed to say? If I tell them how I really feel, shoot straight, they can't print it anyhow.' The unreality of it all was daunting, and Mitchum must have wondered what effect it was all having on his personality. Of course he denied it was having any. 'People say I've changed, but I haven't,' he told Hedda Hopper. It was other people's reaction to him that had changed. 'The other day I went into a store to buy a present for my wife and got the brush-off until one of the sales-girls recognised me. Then they all but handed me the store. Now if, for example, I fail to speak to a doorman, people say, "See Mitchum? He's gone high hat since he hit pay dirt in the movies. Won't speak to a doorman, eh?" Well, five years ago I wouldn't have spoken to him either, and what's more he wouldn't have spoken to me. He wouldn't have let me into the joint . . .'

But despite the sense of all this, the doubts must have persisted. He never seemed to tire of telling reporters that he'd never 'go Hollywood'. And there was always the fear that one morning he'd wake up to find that it was all over. 'Nice going at the moment,' he told Marjorie Williams in 1948, 'but don't think I don't realise I'm here between trains.' That simple piece of common sense may have concealed a mountain of insecurity.

The crisis, when it came, would come out of his 'private' life. In the magazine articles he came across as the happy family man, with the sweet, adoring wife and the requisite brace of lovely children. Dorothy was interviewed too, and she waxed lyrical about her man's cooking ability and amiable usefulness around the house. The truth, however, was both more and less mundane: they were an ordinary family, facing both the usual problems and the extraordinary pressures imposed by Mitchum's public position and wealth. Dorothy not only had the children 'running all over her', she also had to cope with her husband's fame, family and friends. The family, it seems from odd facts and hints, was not as much in love with her as Mitchum was, and the friends, mostly ex-army buddies whom Mitchum seems to have used to counterbalance the unreality of his professional life, became more and more of a problem as his star rose. He became famous as a soft touch.

Mitchum, as the focus of all this factional rivalry for his attention, seems to have tried to please everyone and offend no one. It was an impossible task, and it also laid him wide open to exploitation. This was realised by his 'best friend' and 'business manager', Paul Behrman, who late in 1947 admitted that he couldn't explain the disappearance of most of the star's earnings. The star must have spent it all himself, Behrman claimed. Mitchum denied this—a 'monstrous falsity' he later called it—but he wouldn't prosecute Behrman.

Unfortunately his mother and sister seem to have taken his refusal to do so as evidence of guilt, and set about persuading him to see a psychiatrist. He, obliging to the point of absurdity, agreed, and the psychiatrist duly told him that he was suffering from 'over-amiability', an inability to say no. Soon after this the family went to Delaware for a visit, and Dorothy refused to return to Hollywood with her husband. According to Tomkies she had already told friends that 'Bob has gone Hollywood and I can't take it or the people he associates with.' Mitchum, questioned on the state of his marriage by the ever-eager press, said: 'While it's not true that we are separated, it's nevertheless true that she prefers New York to Hollywood and wants to live there. But I work in Hollywood and can't find it possible to do as she seeks – move to the East.'

The way things were going the over-amiable Mitchum was going to end up pleasing nobody. He was clearly a troubled man at this time, and one means of easing the tension was at hand – marijuana. Parrish, in his book *The Tough Guys*, writes that the actor began using the drug occasionally in 1947 as a way to settle his nerves. Daniel Mainwaring offered some confirmation of this, claiming that on the set of *Out of the Past* Mitchum was smoking dope 'all the time'.

On his return from Delaware in June 1948 he discovered that the film he'd come back for was a non-starter, and that he had plenty of time on his hands. Rather than brood on the future of his marriage he set about converting the house into flats for sale, so that Dorothy, if she came back, could have the bigger house she wanted. He also spent a lot of time at the beach and more time than he should have done drinking. And one evening in August he had the misfortune to find himself in the same room as two policemen and a fistful of joints.

4 Problems, Problems

With Jane Greer and Kirk Douglas in *Out of the Past*, 1947

'An admirer of mine once asked my wife what I represent to the public. She said, "Sex". Finished the conversation.'

(Mitchum, *c* 1958)

THE BACKGROUND to, and the events of, the police raid on Lila Leeds' house that night have never been fully verified. According to the police report the dramatic entrance of Detective-Sergeant Alva Barr and Sergeant J. B. McKinnon represented the culmination of eight months' investigatory work. They'd been watching Mitchum, among others, ever since receiving information that he was a marijuana-user, and though they hadn't expected him to show up that night—that was just a 'lucky break'—his days had been clearly numbered.

Just who it was that they were expecting, as they waited patiently in the garden, has never been revealed, but when Mitchum arrived they recognised him 'immediately', and

With Jane Greer in *Out of the Past*, 1947

through the open window observed him offer a cigarette packet to Miss Leeds and her friend Vicki Evans. The latter asked, 'Gee, what will it do to me? And what happens if it knocks me out?' 'Oh daddy', Mitchum allegedly replied.

The two policemen then tried to enter the premises. Two dogs were enticed out of the way—'we played with them and they went out'—but the kitchen door was unfortunately hooked from the inside. The force was obviously with them, however; Vicki Evans, hearing a scuffling noise, thought it was the dogs seeking admittance, and went to open the door. Bursting into the living-room the two officers found Mitchum and his friend Robin Ford both holding cigarettes, and swiftly foiled clumsy attempts to dispose of them. Gathering such evidence together they then invited the foursome to accompany them to the local constabulary. The press was already there, but the police denied any knowledge of who had tipped them off.

Mitchum's version of the day's events was somewhat different. He had spent most of the day house-hunting with Robin Ford, the estate-agent friend who had first introduced him to Lila Leeds. He had dated the aspiring actress at least once, but had since decided that their relationship should go no further. On the way home from their house-hunting Ford had phoned Leeds, and back at Mitchum's home Leeds had phoned Ford, spoken to Mitchum, and invited both men up to see her new house. Mitchum had been reluctant, saying he had a script to read, but later that evening the two men had gone out to look for food, and after making several more phone calls to unknown persons, Ford had finally persuaded Mitchum that they should drop in on the actress for a few minutes. Mitchum seems once again to have been unable to say no.

At the house, Mitchum claimed in his eventual probation plea, 'we were met at the door by Miss Leeds and two affectionate boxer puppies which Miss Leeds described as "ferocious", to the general amusement. Another girl entered the room, and Miss Leeds introduced her as Vicki Evans. I remarked that I thought someone was outside the house and I went to the front windows to look out. Seeing nothing, I crossed the room and sat down on the couch. Miss Leeds crossed over and handed me a cigarette and upon accepting it, I looked up and saw what I believed to be a face at the window. I said, "There's a face at the window." Miss Evans said, "It's those damn dogs," and ran into the kitchen. At that moment there was a loud crash and two men burst into the room, holding Miss Evans as a shield. Without bothering to drop the cigarette, I crouched to throw one small table at the men, thinking it was a hold-up, and at the same time one of them shouted, "Police officers!" and moved towards me. Realising that I had burned my fingers, I released the cigarette and rubbed my sore fingers on the couch. Sergeant Barr retrieved the cigarette and moved across the room to Miss Leeds. Not wishing any further moves misinterpreted, I offered my wrist to Officer McKinnon, who had already handcuffed Ford. I observed cigarettes in a crumpled Philip Morris wrapper on the table, and pushed them over towards Barr. He attempted to thrust the packet into my hands, and said, "These are yours." I replied they were not, and he said, "Look, don't give me any business, and we'll get along fine."'

Twenty-five years later Mitchum would paint the scene more colourfully. Arriving at the Leeds house, 'the minute I walked in I went sniff-sniff, and the place was *hot*, man. I walked over to pick up the phone and somebody said, "Where you goin'?" I said, "Ah-hah, a lotta heat in this joint. What're those two faces at the window?" And those goddamn dogs— *bam*! Down came the door and I went uh-oh. One of the cops yelled, "Mitchum is raising his arm in a threatening manner." I said, "Hang me up, boys—I been had." Slightly *yentzed*. Roundly fucked.'

He'd certainly been had. As he later told Bill Davidson: 'I'd like to know the answer to some pertinent questions. Why were the newspapers tipped off, before I even arrived at the Leeds house, that a big-name movie star was going to be picked up on a marijuana charge that night? Why did Robin Ford stop off to make so many phone calls that night? Why didn't the police raid the Leeds house earlier, since they testified they had seen Leeds smoking long before I arrived? Why did Vicki Evans go to the kitchen door just before the police broke in, and why was she the only one of us who was never convicted? Why did half a dozen other movie stars come up to me later and thank me, saying *they* had been invited to a party at that house that night, but when they arrived it was already surrounded by police cars, lights flashing, so they took off.'

Whether he was actually guilty of the possession and conspiracy charges brought against him was largely irrelevant. As he admitted himself, 'if somebody had handed me a joint to take with me on the road, I might have taken it, so it makes little difference if I was actually guilty or not.' What did matter, at the time, was that somebody had set out to get him, and had succeeded. The consequences were not likely to be pleasant.

Down at the station he gave his occupation as 'former

Overleaf: With Greer Garson, with whom he was to make *Desire Me*, 1947

actor', and was quoted as saying, 'I'm ruined, I'm all washed up in pictures now, I guess. This is the living end.' He was then examined by a police psychiatrist. 'They brought me there in shackles—me and the other peons. I'm sitting there stark naked and the doctor comes in and says, "How are you?" "I'm fine", I said, "how are you?" Then came the questions: Do you go to parties? Yes, I do. What do you do there? I get drunk, follow pretty broads, make a fool of myself, stagger home. Do you ever go to parties with men? Yes. What do you do? Talk dirty, play poker, get drunk. Do you like pretty girls? Yeah. Do you go out with them? No. Why not? Because my wife won't let me.'

Dorothy's reaction was probably uppermost in his mind. The marriage had been sailing through stormy waters before this contretemps with the laws of the land, and Mitchum must have feared that it was now on the rocks. But newsmen informed him that Dorothy was at this moment returning cross-country from Delaware. Might there be a reconciliation, they asked. Mitchum told them he'd like to think so, but that his wife was 'a very resolute woman'.

The next morning all four 'bustees' were released on bail. They found that the American press was having a field-day, with three-inch-deep headlines, a few facts and a wealth of innuendo. The story, as far as the media was concerned, had everything: drugs, crime, drama, immorality, a whiff of adultery and one famous film star. Photographs of Mitchum, looking suitably traumatised by his arrest, adorned the newsstands.

The police were enjoying themselves too. 'We are going to clean the dope and the narcotic sellers out of Hollywood, and we don't care whom we have to arrest', trumpeted hero-of-the-hour Alva Barr. They had 'a number of other important and prominent screen personalities under surveillance'; Hollywood could 'let this serve as a warning'. The hills were alive to the sound of flushing loos.

Others had less reason to be sanguine. RKO's shares dropped an eighth of a point on the stock exchange, and it was estimated that the studio had more than $1,250,000 invested in unreleased Mitchum pictures. Throwing their star to the wolves was too expensive to contemplate. Instead, the company and David Selznick, who shared ownership of Mitchum's contract, offered an optimistic statement to the hungry press: 'All the facts of the case are not yet known. We urgently request members of the industry and the public to withhold its judgement until these facts are known. Both studios feel confident the American people will not permit Mr Mitchum's prominence in the motion picture industry to deprive him of the rights and privileges of every American citizen to fair play.'

They also got Mitchum a lawyer. Jerry Giesler was no stranger to Hollywood cases, having defended Chaplin against a paternity suit and Flynn against a rape charge. He was also a winner—not one of the 70 clients he had defended on murder charges had been executed. Mitchum could hardly have hoped for better legal representation.

More help was on the way. Early in the morning of September 3, 1948, Dorothy and the two boys arrived home, and it was immediately made clear that she intended to stand by her man. 'Everybody ought to be able to see that Bob is a sick man,' she told the assembled press corps, 'otherwise he'd never be mixed up in a situation like this. Our differences were the same all married couples get into. We have now made them up. I love my husband and am now back to stay with him. I'm indignant, though, that not only Bob but our whole family should have to suffer simply because he is a motion picture star. Otherwise I don't think all this fuss would have been made just because a man may have got mixed up with bad company.'

On the same day another statement was issued by the Selznick studio, with Mitchum's employers confidently expecting 'that when the facts are fully understood and reported, there will be an end to the mental anguish that is being suffered by Mr Mitchum and his family, and that his place in the affections of the country's millions of theatregoers will be untouched.'

The Grand Jury which listened to the police evidence proved singularly immune to Dorothy's pleadings or the studio's sob-story, indicting Mitchum and the other three on possession and conspiracy to possess charges. Superior Court Judge Ambrose arraigned them all for trial on 21 September, but the day of judgement was to be twice delayed, once at Giesler's request and once because the lawyer ran his car into an innocent palm tree. Mitchum and Leeds were finally tried on 10 January 1949.

Mitchum didn't plead guilty or innocent, didn't in fact plead anything. Giesler had decided that a Not Guilty plea would involve a jury trial, 'with the D.A. grilling everyone concerned and digging for dirt'; instead he proposed 'simply to ask the court to decide his innocence or guilt on the conspiracy-to-possess-marijuana count on the basis only of the transcript of the testimony before the grand jury.'

This was the best available option because the conspiracy charge, unlike the possession charge, did not carry a mandatory jail sentence on conviction—Mitchum might get away with probation. He put in a lengthy plea for such leniency, admitting that he had used marijuana in the past while denying the police version of the events in question. But he had transgressed, and the 'millions of pages of ugly black newsprint' had 'shocked' him into realising the 'enormity' of the 'transgression'. He would not, 'at any time whatsoever', use marijuana again.

The judge, after taking a month to consider sentence, found himself unable to agree with Mitchum's feeling that 'time in jail would add nothing to the subjective feeling I already have about what I have done'. The actor had a responsibility to the 'hundreds of thousands of young Americans' who idolised him, and justice had to be seen to be done. Both Mitchum and Leeds received a suspended one year sentence and two years probation, the first sixty days of which would be spent in the County jail.

Meanwhile, the 'hundreds of thousands' were busy demonstrating their support for the star. RKO released *Rachel and the Stranger* to test the waters, and the response was overwhelming, with audiences cheering Mitchum each time he appeared. The film went on to be one of the studio's biggest hits of the year. The judge might have decided the battle, but Mitchum, it seemed, had won the war for survival as a star. He was able to receive his sentence with dignity, and to joke with newsmen about forgetting his toothbrush.

The studio bosses were delighted with the way things were going. Selznick announced that 'Bob will come out of his troubles a finer man who will go on to even greater success', and a letter from an RKO executive to a 'friend' in London, which just happened to get leaked, observed that Mitchum, despite his indiscretion, was 'very popular with us all', being 'as little changed by success as any star I have ever met'. 'No doubt,' the writer piously added, 'he will accept this as a lesson and be guided accordingly in the future.'

While all this grease was being applied to the publicity machines Mitchum was settling down to life as Prisoner 91234. For the first twenty-seven days of his sentence he mopped floors, wrote letters and played cards in the County Jail. Conversations, he told newsmen, revolved around their lives of crime. He was obviously popular with his fellow inmates, being elected a trusty just before he was moved to an outside prison, Honor Farm, for the rest of his sixty days. There he milked a cow for the assembled photographers, before starting

Rachel and the Stranger, 1948

72

regular work in the prison's cement factory.

He claimed to have enjoyed his stay. His insomnia had been cured, and he'd managed to get some privacy at last. 'It was a relief to get away for a while. It's been the finest vacation I've had in seven years . . . I have never felt better in my life.' It had been 'like Palm Springs—without the riff-raff'.

Many years later he told Grover Lewis that life inside had been more problematic than he'd claimed. 'As a matter of fact, they tried to set me up again in there. They wanted to make me for the whole deuce. They didn't want to be wrong. I don't know which side of the fuzz it was, but somebody told me, "Watch it, they're trying to make you, rack you up in the joint." I said fuck it, put me in an individual cell . . . it was the only thing to do when I found out they were manoeuvring against me, planting me with stoolies and all that kind of shit. Man, they can do anything they want you know, charge you with some minor infraction of the rules, and you end up doing two big ones in Quentin . . . Fortunately, there were enough guys on my side who said, "Wait a minute—what're you trying to do to this asshole? Why're you trying to break his balls?"'

On his release Mitchum announced that he was 'through with my so-called pals', that he had 'gained a vast amount of experience'. 'Most men,' he thought, 'got into trouble from selfishness and prolonged adolescence. This has been a milestone in my life.' He probably meant it too. But whilst in jail he had not learned any new respect for the authorities, who had set him up in the first place and then tried to do it again. Self-improvement was one thing, becoming a model citizen something else entirely.

The full story of Mitchum's bust, of who set him up with whose help and why, will probably never be revealed. It seems likely that Robin Ford and Vicki Evans were implicated, whether willingly or not, and it seems certain that the police were in the market for a famous scalp. Mitchum later claimed that his ex-business manager, who had sworn vengeance on the star at his own trial, had been one of the set-up's prime organisers.

The authorities were soon investigating the rumours that his prosecution had been carefully arranged, and the District Attorney's office eventually set up a full investigation. It reported in January 1951, declined to publicise its findings, but ordered that the guilty verdict 'be set aside and that a plea of not guilty be entered and that the information or complaint be dismissed'.

Mitchum didn't go out of his way to spread the news of the quashed verdict. Perhaps he felt tired of the whole business, perhaps he felt that, in the end, it had done his career more good than harm. In this he was probably right. The columnists had decided to follow the fans and use Mitchum's bust as proof of his larger-than-lifeness. 'With Bob a miracle happened,' wrote Alan Warwick, 'the case and his sentence of sixty days produced no sort of visible contrary effect on his career as a film star. Rather, it established the heart-warming fact that Bob has an army of supporters to stand by him when things go wrong. That is a quite remarkable reponse to a man who had never got nearer to his followers than the cinema screen. In other words, Bob Mitchum seems to have what it needs to project himself—frailties and all—clean through the celluloid that stretches between him and those who think he's got something.'

During the years 1947–9 Robert Mitchum was not the only one having problems: Hollywood as a whole was going through the first of its post-war crises. The boom year of 1946 had turned out to be a one-off, giving way to the more lasting spectre of cinematic decline.

For one thing the success of the immediate post-war year had proved a two-edged sword, encouraging those who worked in the industry to demand their share of the booming receipts. A series of strikes in 1945–6 produced a 25 per cent hike in earnings for many studio employees, and in the less successful years that followed these employees proved understandably reluctant to lower their expectations accordingly. Between 1944 and 1948 Hollywood's overall production costs doubled.

A second blow descended in 1947. Britain, after giving some consideration to nationalisation of the cinema industry, decided instead to tax Hollywood's British earnings at a swingeing 75 per cent rate, and at the requisite stroke of trade secretary Harold Wilson's pen Hollywood's entire foreign earnings were slashed by more than half. It was time for an economy drive, and since cutting the workforce was easier than cutting wages thousands were thrown out of work. For those still employed by the studios the whole atmosphere of movie-making began to change. Budget-cutting demanded less on-set spontaneity, so rehearsals replaced continuous takes and rigid scripts were preferred to improvisation. The movies themselves changed: stories which required expensive sets, thousands of extras or extensive location shooting were no longer financially viable. Deprived of its hereditary right to glossiness, Hollywood was forced towards a low-budget realism out of sheer financial necessity. Small psychological melodramas were the new order of the day, shot either indoors or at night (when the sets looked less obvious), and labelled 'quality pictures'. Quantity would have been preferable, but it cost too much.

Another blow was delivered by the witch-hunters, when some bright spark on the House of UnAmerican Activities Committee realised how vulnerable Hollywood was to the enemies of freedom. Communist movies—what better way could the foe find to subvert the American dream? When ten prominent members of the film community refused to say whether they were or had been communists, pleading the Fifth Amendment, the studio bosses surrendered to the prevailing paranoia and announced that they'd take the responsibility for cleaning up Hollywood. The blacklist was drawn up, depriving many of their livelihood and costing the movie industry some of its most talented people. Two of the Ten, Dmytryk and Scott, had been the director and producer of RKO's *Crossfire*.

While all this hysterical nonsense was being whipped up by hysterical idiots the industry was under increasing threat from a far greater enemy than communism—television. By 1949 40 per cent of the American public would have access to the box, would be able to watch the mainstream entertainment, which Hollywood had traditionally offered, in the comfort of their own living-rooms.

One man, Floyd Odlum, concluded that the jig was up in so far as movies were concerned, and he happened to own a controlling stake in RKO. He sold out to Howard Hughes, legendary wonderboy of both aviation and the cinema.

Hughes had inherited his father's multimillion dollar company at the age of eighteen, and through the twenties and thirties had taken it to even greater heights. He was reckoned to be a mechanical genius, designing planes and anything else that needed designing at the drop of a hat. He had broken trans-oceanic flying records and created Trans World Airline. He had also made movies, won a director's Oscar at the age of twenty-two and gone on to make some of the most popular movies of the early thirties, before turning his attention back to aviation.

It was not until 1940 that he directed again, taking over from Howard Hawks on his pet project, *The Outlaw*. This was supposedly a western, but the plot and the sagebrush settings were little more than convenient back-drops for displaying the

Blood on the Moon, 1948

76

ample charms of Hughes' latest discovery, Jane Russell. Not surprisingly the film ran into censorship trouble, and was not released until 1943. It did little business, and Hughes quickly withdrew it from circulation, reckoning that time and the censors were on his side. A Baltimore judge duly observed that 'Miss Russell's breasts hung over the picture like a summer thunderstorm spread out over the landscape—they were everywhere', and when the picture was re-released in 1946 it made a fortune.

During this film's long history Hughes had also been pursuing his myriad other interests, notably designing and producing a giant flying boat for the government and adding to his collection of starlets whom he intended, one day, to groom for stardom. Perhaps they provided one reason for his acquisition of RKO, but if so, he seems to have soon regretted his decision, muttering that the company was a 'damned nuisance', representing 15 per cent of his business yet taking 85 per cent of his time.

Dore Schary was still production chief when Hughes took over as owner, and he was told by his new boss that he'd have complete freedom of decision on the artistic side. Two months later he resigned, complaining about Hughes' continual interference. The boss had cancelled two of Schary's most favoured projects, one of which, *Battleground*, would become MGM's second highest revenue earner of 1949.

But, rightly or wrongly, Hughes' reasons for getting rid of Schary were clear enough. Quite apart from any doubts he may have entertained as to the latter's political reliability—a prime consideration at this time—Hughes felt he knew what the American public wanted, and it wasn't psychology and social comment. One woman and two men, preferably in an exotic location—that was the formula for success. The men had to be beefy, stoical types, the women had to have breasts that looked luscious from any conceivable angle. The dialogue had to be adult, as befitted movies which brought sex close to the romantic surface. Hughes had a theory which he once explained to Mitchum—'the public is secretly convinced that the leading man is always having an affair with his leading lady. And that's why they go to the theatre—in the hope of catching them at it.'

Nothing throws more light on Hughes' approach to the art of cinema than a memo he sent to RKO studio manager C. J. Tevlin in 1951. The subject-matter was a dress specially made for Jane Russell, which she would wear in one short scene of *Macao*. It was made of silver-gold mesh lamé, weighed twenty-six pounds, and was reportedly adjusted with pliers. 'This dress is terrific and should be used, by all means,'

78

Hughes wrote. 'However the fit of the dress around her breasts is not good and gives the impression, God forbid, that her breasts are padded or artificial. They just don't appear to be in natural contour. It looks as if she is wearing a brassière of some very stiff material which does not take the contour of her breasts . . . I am not recommending that she go without a brassière, as I know this is a very necessary piece of equipment for Russell. But I thought, if we could find a half-brassière which will support her breasts upward and still not be noticeable under the dress, or alternatively, a very thin brassière made of very thin material so that the natural contour of her breasts will show through the dress, it will be a great deal more effective . . . Now, it would be extremely valuable if the brassière, or the dress, incorporated some kind of a point at the nipple because I know this does not ever occur naturally in the case of Jane Russell. Her breasts always appear to be round, or flat, at that point so something artificial here would be extremely desirable if it could be incorporated without destroying the contour of the rest of her breasts . . . You understand that all the comment immediately above is with respect to the dress made of metallic cloth. However, the comment is equally applicable to any other dress she wears, and I would like these instructions followed with respect to all of her wardrobe . . . I want the rest of her wardrobe, wherever possible, to be low-necked (and by that I mean as low as the law allows) so that customers can get a look at the part of Russell which they pay to see . . .'

This memo was typical of Hughes' approach in more ways than one: the fact that its contents were communicated in writing was significant in itself. Hughes had an office at the Sam Goldwyn studio, and he never bothered to get one at the RKO lot. He is alleged to have visited the new studio only once, then uttering his immortal 'paint it', but it is more likely that he never went there at all. He was quite able to interfere by memo and telephone, and notoriously hard to contact when a decision was needed which he didn't want to take. 'Working for Hughes', according to one of the RKO management team, was 'like taking the ball in a football game and running four feet, only to find the coach tackling you from behind.'

For Mitchum, Hughes' takeover was to prove very much a mixed blessing. Initially he had good reason to be grateful: Hughes could easily have dumped the actor after the drug-bust affair, citing the morals clause with ample legal justification, but instead he went out of his way to be helpful. He bought out Selznick's share of Mitchum's contract, loaned him $50,000 for his legal expenses, even hired a private eye to keep a watch over the trouble-prone star. This was partly sound business—Mitchum's beefy masculinity, insolent sexuality and way with one-liners made him an ideal foil for Hughes' heroines—but the RKO boss also seems to have liked the actor on a personal level, perhaps recognising him as a fellow maverick in Hollywood's largely conformist world. Mitchum later remembered one of Hughes' back-handed compliments: 'Robert, you're like a pay toilet, aren't you? You don't give a shit for nothing.'

On the debit side Mitchum was now tied, by contract and the need to pay back the loan—which was being deducted from his salary—to a studio committed to the making of unadventurous movies. There would be no *Pursued*, no *Locket*, no *Out of the Past*, during Hughes' reign at RKO, just a string of routine programmes carved out according to the boss's formula. In the process of making them, Mitchum's cynical attitude towards movies and his own career in them would harden, becoming as much a matter of belief as a device for self-preservation. If, in 1948, Mitchum did 'give a shit' for anything to do with movies, his last five years at RKO would go a long way towards making Hughes' comment a self-fulfilling prophecy.

Mitchum in court, 1949

5 The Straining Bodice as Art

The Big Steal, 1949

'At RKO I became, along with Jane Russell's bust, one of Howard Hughes' biggest assets.'

(Mitchum, 1979)

MITCHUM'S FIRST post-jail movie had an interesting history. Apparently Hughes picked the mouldering script of *The Big Steal* off a shelf at RKO (how he managed this without visiting the place is unknown) as a vehicle for Mitchum whilst the actor was marooned between indictment and trial. If he had a film in production, so Hughes reasoned, it could be shown that his jailing would adversely affect all those others involved in the project. The ploy failed, but the decision to make the film during Mitchum's trial and subsequent imprisonment would leave its mark on the finished product.

Lizabeth Scott was the first choice for leading lady, but she pulled out, fearing that association with such a disreputable

Holiday Affair, 1949

character would harm her career. Jane Greer, brought in as a replacement, was 'eager to work with him again', but 'not mad about the script'. Director Don Siegel shared her opinion, and freely admitted that 'it was an excuse to get Robert Mitchum out of jail'. The story was 'incredibly bad', 'the whole thing was done tongue-in-cheek, and none of us took it very seriously'.

Mitchum was involved in shooting before and after his incarceration, with Siegel filming the long chase sequence in the intervening period, patching in the close-ups at a later date. 'If you look closely at the film,' he observed later, 'you can see that when Mitchum arrives at certain places there are leaves on the trees, and when Bendix arrives moments later the leaves are gone.' He also remembered Mitchum's arrival on-set after his release: 'Mitchum showed up absolutely out cold, having drunk a bottle and a half of tequila with his probation officer, who if anything was drunker than Mitchum.' The location, needless to say, was situated in the heart of Mexico's marijuana-growing area.

Despite all these tribulations, *The Big Steal* turned out quite well. Siegel's slam-bang style of direction made the most of the chase sequences, and Mitchum and Greer offered a few reminders of how good they were at exchanging laconic utterances. The *Monthly Film Bulletin* reviewer thought it 'an unpretentious, enjoyable and fast-moving thriller of the kind that one seldom sees nowadays'; Hughes would doubtless have felt thoroughly vindicated by such an appraisal. Mitchum, when asked his opinion, offered his usual, caustic form of resignation: 'I didn't like *The Big Steal*, but it's making a barrel of money, so I'll be doing *The Big Steal* from now on.'

Well, almost. First he had to charm his way through *Holiday Affair*, which also got good contemporary reviews. *Variety* thought it one of Mitchum's 'best acting stints', despite the 'type switch', and the *New York Herald Tribune* agreed. 'Mitchum is really working out of his usual territory,' the scribe opined, 'he does extremely well.' In more recent times this film has been somewhat down-graded—in his cinematic encyclopaedia David Thomson dismisses it as a 'sentimental comedy'—but for once the first impression seems to have been more accurate. *Holiday Affair* may be 'sentimental comedy', but it's also something more, and Mitchum's role, though superficially outside his usual territory, is tailor-made for the persona he was then, albeit unconsciously, developing.

With Faith Domergue in *Where Danger Lives*, 1950

Overleaf: With Jane Russell in *His Kind of Woman*, 1951

The plot revolves around the familiar love triangle. A war widow with a young son is being pressured into marrying a suitor, and since her prime interest lies in keeping her husband's memory alive a suitor that she doesn't love seems a good bet. Enter Mitchum, a nice, rather anarchistic alternative, whom she responds to in the way that she responded to her husband. Eventually she admits as much to herself.

While this triangle is being resolved the participants get involved in some delightful comic situations, and also manage to swap some observations on human relationships which seem unusually wise for a Hollywood movie. Mitchum's character is wonderfully eccentric, sharing his lunch with the seals in the park, sharing Christmas gifts with a tramp, amazingly direct in his relations with the woman, her child and the world in general. If, all in all, *Holiday Affair* is middle of the road soap, it's a superior example of it, and Mitchum's nonconformist brand of common sense comes like a breath of fresh air in an era of more hidebound romantic heroes.

He was back in more familiar territory with *Where Danger Lives*, a Hughes vehicle *par excellence*. These days it would be called *The Locket 2* or *The Big Steal 2*, but unfortunately neither Laraine Day nor Jane Greer were chosen for the 'sequel'. The new *femme fatale* was Faith Domergue, one of several actresses whom Hughes had been grooming for legendary status. Unfortunately she couldn't act, and *Where Danger Lives* is replete with the evidence.

The plot was particularly lurid. Mitchum, playing the first of his many doctors, falls for wealthy socialite whom he saves from suicide and swiftly dumps his nice girlfriend. He then finds out that the socialite's brother is really her husband. Husband then informs him that she's crazy, but of course he won't believe it. Husband hits him on the head with a convenient poker, then conveniently collapses. Mitchum wakes up to find husband dead—she's killed him but he thinks he has—and the lovers, true to the genre tradition, head for Mexico. Meanwhile the poker-blow has engendered a spreading paralysis, rendering him unable to act on his growing awareness that she really is crazy.

The critics were sympathetic so far as he was concerned, but Faith Domergue got the full treatment. The *Time* reviewer hit the nail on the head, announcing the film as a formula vehicle for 'the latest graduate of Hughes' straining bodice school of dramatic art'.

Worse was to come. Ava Gardner might conceal more acting ability behind her straining bodice than the unfortunate Miss Domergue, but *My Forbidden Past* didn't require her to reveal it. If *Where Danger Lives* remains watchable TV fare on a wet night, the viewer would be better advised to stand out in the rain than watch this appalling inept piece of period soap. The reviewers captured the essence of the film, usually in less than ten words. 'A cloying saccharine saga', said *The New York Times*; 'a screenplay that is hardly distinguished by originality', noted the *Herald Tribune*; 'an unrelievedly sordid film', moaned the *Monthly Film Bulletin.*

It had a fairly sordid genesis. Polan Banks wrote the novel, *Carriage Entrance*, on which it was based, and it was originally intended that he and RKO should co-produce with Anne Sheridan in the starring role. Hughes didn't take to Miss Sheridan, however, and he managed to shelve production until Banks could be forced off the project, and Ava Gardner brought in.

Not that it mattered how good or bad Miss Sheridan was. No actress could do justice to lines like 'Now that I am married I cannot possibly see you again', or breathe life into a character so unrelievedly unpleasant. Mitchum noted that at first he was 'pencilled in as a real square John. We didn't have much of a script to start with, so I suggested that the first scene should be like the climactic scene in *Ecstacy*. I figured that if we were going to give the public a shock treatment, we might as well do it up brown.' His suggestion was ignored, and the cast surrendered to the costumes. The film managed to accumulate $700,000 in losses.

The Racket was produced for equally idealistic reasons: Hughes wanted to cash in on the Kefauver Crime Hearings then under way. The story had originally been filmed as a silent in 1928, but time had not been kind to it; what had once seemed daringly original now, umpteen gangster movies later, seemed tired and stale. The director, John Cromwell, thought the material 'so old hat that I couldn't arouse much interest in it at all'. What acting honours there were for the taking went to Robert Ryan, playing the principal villain. The reviews were almost universally awful, but for once Hughes had the last laugh—*The Racket* was RKO's third highest grosser of 1951.

Either side of *The Racket* Mitchum made his two films with Jane Russell, *His Kind of Woman* and *Macao*. Theirs was an inevitable pairing, and these two movies a triumph for Hughes' low-life romanticism. His top male and female star trade sexual innuendos in front of the most exotic cardboard sets RKO could afford, forcing themselves into mobility only when the villain's machinations make it absolutely unavoidable.

Louella Parsons announced Mitchum and Russell as the 'hottest combination ever to hit the screen', apparently in the hope that Hughes would reinstate her daughter as a producer at RKO, but the sleepiest combination would have been more apt, indeed, the ad campaign for the first film featured the twosome in a position that was anything but vertical. Bogart and Bacall, Tracy and Hepburn, they clearly were not, but Mitchum and Russell did offer something strikingly original, a sleazy alliance of perennial losers, almost invulnerable physically, yet possessed of an emotional strength that was brittle to the point of non-existence. They really worked hard at being indifferent. They needed to.

Both films are striking too, without actually being good. In *His Kind of Woman* a dishevelled Mitchum first encounters Russell, a sheathed body singing a sultry song, at a dishevelled Mexican airport. Naturally they're both headed for the same resort hotel, as is Vincent Price, a movie star on the lam from his wife, who soon has his own encounter with the sheathed body. Mitchum, meanwhile, is playing a proto-Jim Rockford figure, and getting up to his neck in something he doesn't understand. Behind the scenes a pre-Perry Mason Raymond Burr is oilily pulling strings.

There's lots of time for sleepy backchat, however. 'I've got to tell you something about myself,' he says to her. 'One thing about you, you never talk about others,' she replies. He soon draws level in the exchanges. After killing a gangster he presents himself for more dialogue. 'I hear you killed Ferraro,' she says. 'How does it feel?' 'He didn't tell me,' Mitchum murmurs back.

It's a strange film. The first hour is almost absurdist in the *film noir* tradition, with all the participants but the villain resigned to accepting a world in which nothing ever goes right. Mitchum's character has no control over his life and doesn't expect any; he just follows the course of least resistance with an occasional mental shrug. When he discovers that he's to be the human guinea pig in a plastic surgery experiment he's not in the least surprised. Fate is fate.

But then, just as the villains are really getting down to their villainy, the whole mood of the film switches from *noir* to pure farce. Vincent Price takes over, decides he'll be the hero he is in movies, and leads the hotel guests on a mission to rescue Mitchum. Soon the latter is back in his room ironing his

With Jane Russell in *Macao*, 1952

92

money—he always irons when he's bored—and waiting for Russell to drop by with a few more innuendos.

This three-films-in-one got terrible reviews, and for *Macao* the villain was down-graded, the farce written out, and the Mitchum-Russell 'chemistry' pushed out into centre-stage. In fact 'stage' was the operative word, for the bustling port of Macao, den of Oriental iniquity etc., looks about fifty yards long. It probably cost less than the famous metal dress.

Macao didn't suffer from a lack of prestigious directors—it had two. Joseph von Sternberg, whose name through the late thirties was almost synonymous with Marlene Dietrich's exotic romances, had one more movie to make 'in accordance with the RKO contract I had foolishly accepted'. His memories of *Macao* would not be pleasant. It was 'made under the supervision of six different men in charge . . . instead of fingers in that pie, half a dozen clowns immersed various parts of their anatomy in it. Their names do not appear on the list of credits.'

He was finished with the film in the autumn of 1950, but Hughes was not satisfied, and put it on the shelf along with several others he had doubts about. Nicholas Ray was asked to revamp them, and he agreed on condition that the original directors had no objection. Sternberg didn't. Ray then called up all the participants and told them what he wanted to do, among them Gloria Grahame, whom he was currently engaged in divorcing. She watched Sternberg's finished product and offered to waive her alimony if Ray would cut her out entirely.

The basic trouble with *Macao* is that there's nothing much there. The mystery of the Orient consists of one blind Chinese beggar, two thugs in pyjamas and the aforementioned set shrouded in fishing-nets. The story—the sleepy twosome get involved in police attempts to lure a villain out of Macao and into their jurisdiction—is just as thin. All that remains is the twosome's banter, and as a result the villain's main villainy looks like his inability to find appropriate one-liners.

Mitchum and Russell have no such problem. They may be losers, people who get 'lonely on New Year's Eve in Times Square' (him), who are 'looking for something', not knowing 'whether it's a person or a place' (her), but they do know how to swap lines. 'Some girls don't think I'm so bad,' he says winningly. 'Some have bad taste,' she replies crushingly. 'Enjoying the view?' she sneers, as his eyes wander across her contours. 'It ain't the Taj Mahal or the Hanging Gardens of Babylon, but it'll do,' he tells her respectfully.

Jane Russell has not exactly been over-lauded for her acting talent over the years, but in *Macao* she's perfectly in tune with her part and, as *Gentlemen Prefer Blondes* was to show, it was

94

not the only role she could play. Mitchum has no need to raise sweat for his role. It has no complexity, no emotional tone other than amused fatalism, not even much in the way of physical activity. *Macao*, though a watchably mouldy movie in the context of 1984, was, in 1951, evidence of the shoddy use to which Mitchum's talent was being put.

It showed in his personal reviews, which had been going inexorably, if intermittently, downhill. What the critics had called his 'effective deadpan style' in *Crossfire* had become an actor who 'blinks sleepily into space' in *His Kind of Woman*. More and more critics seemed to be consulting Roget's Thesaurus entry 679—Inactivity—when it came to describing a Mitchum performance. The superlatives which had been heaped on *GI Joe*, *Pursued*, *Out of the Past*, even *Holiday Affair*, were becoming rarer and rarer.

Looking back on this period in later years Mitchum admitted to no anxiety about the direction his career was taking, only wry resignation. 'RKO made the same film with me in it for ten years. They were so alike I wore the same suit in six of them and the same Burberry trench coat. They made a male Jane Russell out of me. I was the staff hero. They got so they wanted me to take some of my clothes off in the pictures. I objected to this, so I put on some weight and looked like a Bulgarian wrestler when I took my shirt off. Only two pictures I made in that time made any sense whatever.'

This, of course, was partial nonsense. Many of the films were similar, but the gulf in class between, say, *Pursued* and *My Forbidden Past*, was wide enough for a whole army of Bulgarian wrestlers. When questioned as to *why* he had accepted making the same movie for ten years he would retreat into a well-worn secondary defence system: 'Well, it was better than working. They could never decide to their satisfaction what type I was. One guy would say, "He's a broken-nosed Byronic." Another would say, "No, he ain't, he's an all-American boy." People started talking about Mitchum-type roles, but I still don't know what they mean. They'd paint the eyes on my eyelids man, and I'd walk through it. The least work for the most reward.'

In other words he'd out-criticise the critics, which was one sure way of staying ahead of them, and also, perhaps, an unconscious statement of superiority to the whole wretched business. He humoured them.

Nearer to the period in question, in 1958, he gave a more rounded appraisal. 'At RKO,' he told Thomas Wiseman, 'I did one film after another. They'd tell me, sure, we know the subjects stink, but you're our salesman, we pay you $600 a week to sell this stuff for us. I'd make a token protest once in a while, but I didn't really mind. I made their pictures. That was my job . . .' And the insecurity of such a job, selling other people's rubbish, was quite apparent to him. 'What happens, I asked them, when the public gets tired of going to see me and getting nothing but rubbish from me? Simple, they told me, we get ourselves a new boy. From whom they will take the rubbish.'

At the time, the cynicism was still edged by a real distaste. 'When a studio comes up with a musty old script that brings in the shekels, the actor hasn't got much of an argument,' he said in 1949. 'So I don't bother the studio and it doesn't bother me. Somebody hands me a script, I look at it and ask, "When do I start?" If there is a good story on the lot, you've got to smuggle it out to read it . . .' When he was interested, he told Hedda Hopper, he knew his own lines and everybody else's. When he wasn't he simply arrived on-set and asked what he was supposed to say. 'If you want my interest, interest me. If you just want my presence, pay me.'

He had nothing against rubbish *per se*, but he did object to it being revered. 'Often they embarrass me by saying "we think it's fine". If they said to me, "It stinks but let's make it", then I'm with them. I ain't here because I'm displaying any facility or versatility.' He claimed he never fought for a good story because 'it's a dead cinch you're a loser'. When Hedda Hopper asked him why they didn't give him good stories in the first place, he referred her to the 'typical Mitchum fan . . . glazed eyes, hasn't shaved—who needs it?'

So, a bewildering mixture of statements, which must have reflected the actor's own confused feelings about his work. It paid well, gave him a good living, involved a lot of fun. It was better than working. He'd have liked to be more 'interested' in the films and, presumably, though he never said so in so many words, would have liked to make 'better' films. But, since the way the industry was set up made this profoundly difficult, he was prepared to let his inertia carry him forward. His instinctive feeling that acting was a 'ridiculous and humiliating profession' would then be confirmed by the 'rubbishy' end-product. Many of the films were pretty dire, but to round off Mitchum's self-justification all of them, in retrospect, had to be dreadful.

But this was only part of the story. He might arrive on-set

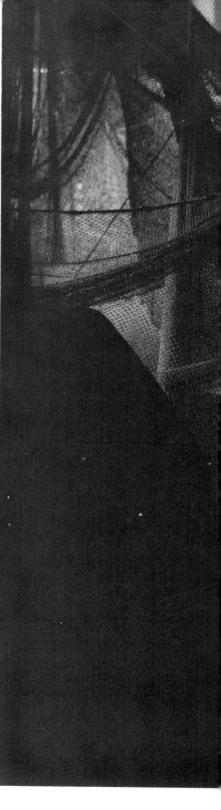

Macao, 1952

Overleaf: With Susan Hayward and Arthur Kennedy
in *The Lusty Men*, 1952

96

and ask for directions like the 'workhorse' he claimed to be, but nearly all the actors and directors who actually worked with him paid testament to his exemplary professionalism. His indifference to the product obviously didn't make him indifferent to the standard of his own work. And when it came to selling rubbish there were limits to what even he would tolerate, as his last years at RKO would show.

Mitchum had always sworn that he'd never 'go Hollywood', and in most respects he'd been true to his word. He went to the studio the way he'd gone to Lockheed, clocked in and clocked out, and went home to his family, to being Dorothy's husband and his children's father. As a family they seem to have had few contacts with the movie community. 'I don't know many stars socially,' he told Aline Mosby in February 1952. 'They don't seek me out either. They've all got Cadillacs and buy their suits at Eddie Schmidt's and they've got time to play. I guess I don't. In fact, I don't know anybody socially. I have a sign on my gate—no peddlers, actors or agents allowed.'

Away from the family, at the studio or on location, he seems to have rather enjoyed the company of his fellow actors. The work was often great fun, and when it wasn't Mitchum was quite prepared to take the responsibility for enlivening the proceedings. Besides finding new names for his co-stars he seemed to take a boyish delight in pretending that he didn't know his lines. Jane Greer fell for this trick, which probably wasn't even aimed at her. 'Bob used to ask "What are the lyrics?" of the script before rehearsing the scene. This lulled me into thinking I too could learn the dialogue under the drier in make-up. I soon found out that he was letter-perfect while I was fumbling around for the words.' Henry Hathaway, directing *White Witch Doctor*, had a similar comedown. When Mitchum walked onto the set and asked what he was supposed to say, Hathaway blew up, shouting 'We've got six pages to shoot and you don't even know your lines?' Mitchum repeated his question more than once, finally pleading 'Will somebody please bring me the script so I can find out *which* scene by the rock this is?' Someone obliged, and after a quick glance Mitchum announced himself ready to go. He was, of course, letter-perfect. Hathaway, who hadn't worked with him before, was amazed. 'Bob, you're the most wonderful guy I ever worked with in my life,' he is reported to have said. 'What do you want for these prices,' Mitchum replied, 'bums?'

But he didn't allow his love of horseplay to get in the way of helping any co-stars who needed it. Greer found him 'so considerate', Margaret Sheridan, the second female lead in *One Minute to Zero*, said 'he was always helping the little fellow. When I started on the picture, I was terribly nervous because my first dialogue scene was with Bob. I knew well that I was going to blow my first line. Bob sensed it too, and before I could fluff he blew his line with a very amusing ad lib that eased the tension, particularly mine.'

Jean Simmons, making her first American picture *Angel Face*, also had reason to thank him. Stewart Granger, who was then Simmons' husband, remembered that 'Bob really took Jean under his wing and, in spite of the bullying of Otto Preminger who was directing it, Jean enjoyed the film. She adored Mitchum and used to tell me what a good actor he was, how funny and amusing and easy-going, he just wouldn't let things get him down . . . In one scene Bob was supposed to smack Jean, and she told the very gentle Mitchum to really let go. Otto insisted on take after take and poor Jean's cheek was getting redder and redder. As Otto insisted on yet another take, Mitchum turned to him and let him have one right across the face. "Would you like another, Otto?" he asked. Otto quickly agreed to print the last take.'

But Mitchum was not without his own survival instinct as an actor-star. If there was one thing he wouldn't allow it was anyone underplaying him. 'Anyone who attempted to do so,' Jane Greer pointed out, 'quickly found they were in trouble. Mitchum would start mumbling, and the soundman would stop the take.' Nobody was going to look more relaxed on screen than Robert Mitchum.

In the six films he made between *Macao* and the expiry of his RKO contract he did not, with one notable exception, have much else to do but look relaxed. RKO was stuck in a rut and Mitchum was stuck at RKO.

One Minute to Zero was a truly dreadful production, a Korean war movie in which Korea seemed only slightly bigger than the company's Macao. It was produced, needless to say, to cash in on the current war, and such details as a credible script seem to have been forgotten in the rush to get it out. The plot featured routine war heroics and the hero's relations with an older woman; unfortunately the older woman hired, Claudette Colbert, dropped out at the last moment, only to be replaced by Ann Blyth, a palpably younger woman. Nobody bothered to revise the script accordingly, and the story made even less sense than before. The one point of interest involved a scene in which Mitchum orders the shelling of civilian

refugees whom he believes are harbouring the enemy. The Defence department took exception to this (the scene, not the reality), and Hughes, true to form, refused to excise it. Any publicity was good publicity and *One Minute to Zero* needed all the help it could get.

The Lusty Men was almost unique in being an excellent film made under Hughes' regime at RKO. Though based on the usual two-men-after-one-woman formula, its setting in the rodeo world of the modern West marked it out as an original, one of the earliest contemporary westerns. In Nicholas Ray the film had a director with few equals in making hard-edged dramatic features, and the script, by ex-cowboy David Dotort and Horace McCoy, both of whom spent several months doing research on the rodeo circuit, proved refreshingly authentic.

Mitchum played Jeff McCloud, a penniless, over-the-hill rodeo champion in search of a less bruising life-style. But he can't escape so easily, getting a ranch job with the help of Wes (Arthur Kennedy) only to find that his helper dreams of being a rodeo star. He and wife Louise (Susan Hayward) want a home of their own, and to him at least rodeo winnings look the ideal short-cut. Jeff half-reluctantly adopts this protégé, who proves remarkably successful.

He also proves unable to stop making money and milking glory once he's reached the original target, and as he becomes increasingly impervious to Louise's anxious pleadings a 'love triangle' threatens to emerge. It takes Jeff's sacrificial death to set him straight and save his marriage.

In its peripherals—the action sequences, two great comic performances by Burt Mustin and Arthur Hunnicut, the settings (one ghastly backdrop excepted), the general ambience of rodeo life—*The Lusty Men* comes close to perfection, but when attention is focused on the central characters there is less cause for total satisfaction. Mitchum's and Hayward's characters are both beautifully understated, but Kennedy's Wes is grossly overdrawn: alternately growling and pouting like a five-year-old he rapidly loses any audience sympathy he might have started with. This is particularly unfortunate in that his seduction by the rodeo world and his wife's reluctance to lose him are the film's two central themes. As it is, it's hard to believe that she chooses him rather than Mitchum. He even says as much at one point.

If *The Lusty Men* proved that Hollywood was not immune to innovation, *Angel Face* proved that imitation was more popu-

With Jean Simmons in *Angel Face*, 1953

103

lar. In this throwback to the forties poor Mitchum once more found himself sucked into disaster by a *femme fatale*, dragged down by a script which might have been written by Freud on a bad day.

The film had the usual discreditable genesis. Otto Preminger was loaned, against his wishes, by Zanuck to Hughes, and presented with a script which he hated. 'Please do not force me to make this film,' he told Hughes, but the RKO boss was adamant. 'My friend, I need you,' he replied. 'Come to my studio tomorrow and you will be like Hitler . . . Whatever you wish will be done.' Preminger insisted on a meeting with Hughes, and this took place, as was the tycoon's practice, in the middle of the night. More of the plot was revealed. 'Jean Simmons, the bitch,' Hughes reportedly hissed, 'she cut her hair short.' The two had apparently had a row and Simmons, with only eighteen days of a loan period to RKO remaining, knowing that Hughes hated short hair on women, had reached for the scissors. What the row had been about no one knew, though Granger later claimed that Hughes had propositioned the actress without success.

Perhaps touched by this sad little tale Preminger agreed to do the movie, and put new writers to work on the screenplay. The story came from 'true life', the Beulah Overell murder trial of 1947, but that didn't make the film seem any more realistic. Simmons played the rich girl who loves her father, hates her stepmother, and uses hapless ambulance driver Mitchum to cover her tracks when she kills the offending woman. The plan goes awry, however, and father is killed too. Mitchum, who's beginning to have doubts about her, nevertheless agrees to the marriage which will save her from prosecution. He then tries to divorce her, and she promptly drives them both off a cliff. At this point, as the *Time* reviewer commented, '*Angel Face* comes to an end, having just about run out of both actors and automobiles.'

The first half of the film is well-developed by Preminger; Simmons' character is slowly revealed to the audience and the tension inexorably mounts. But the second half is far too long, weighted down with poor dialogue, and the audience know the end long before the actors. Both Mitchum and Simmons performed creditably enough, but they were not the 'sizzling love combination burning up the screen' which the publicity spiel claimed. In both *Angel Face* and *She Couldn't Say No* Simmons seems too lightweight an actress for Mitchum, reducing him to the stature of a protective uncle.

The price was still to be paid for *The Lusty Men*, and Mitchum was now loaned to Twentieth Century-Fox to partner Hayward in *White Witch Doctor*, a jungle soap opera. It was his first location stint outside America, though that would be hard to deduce from the film. His question—'which scene by the rock is this?'—encapsulates *White Witch Doctor*, and the only real justification for the film's existence lay in the chance it gave journalists to polish their sarcasm. 'It is not the Africans who need help in this film but the white men,' said the *Monthly Film Bulletin*, 'an amazingly unsurprising romantic adventure,' said the *New York Times*. Mitchum himself was not exempt: the *New Yorker* found him 'dispassionate as a hippo'.

Second Chance had no more to offer in terms of plot, character, dialogue or credibility, but it did have 3D. 'Crashing thrills! Crushing kisses! So real . . . it puts you so close to the lovers you feel everything they feel,' screamed the posters. The last scene, a no-holds-barred fight between Mitchum and Jack Palance on an Andes funicular car, is certainly spectacular, but spectacle, as the movies of the eighties have made clear, is no substitute for story. Mitchum, questioned on-set by Hedda Hopper, was more than usually resigned. 'I hate to say this,' he told her, 'but I honestly don't care.' Besides, there was light at the end of the tunnel—'I've got just one year left with RKO.'

In fact *Second Chance* was to be his last film for the company. *She Couldn't Say No* (*Beautiful but Dangerous* in the UK) had been made earlier, and once more the critics seized their opportunity. The *Time* reviewer noted that three writers had been involved, caustically adding that *War and Peace* had only needed one; the *Newsweek* scribe advised 'students of the art of making next-to-nothing out of virtually nothing' that they might find the film interesting.

Mitchum was a doctor once more, Simmons a rich girl who thinks she owes his small American town a debt for saving her life as a child. She starts distributing gifts anonymously, with disastrous consequences. The town drunk can't cope with quality whisky, the only vet leaves for California, the postman stops delivering mail, etc. In due course an army of money-grabbers descend on the town, demanding their share of the mysterious bounty. All of which could have added up to a funny and pointed film, but it doesn't. The humour is nowhere sharp enough, and *She Couldn't Say No* becomes a watchable but essentially nondescript romantic comedy. Mitchum looks awake enough, but it's not a role which calls for much in the way of acting. As his last-released RKO film it served as a more than adequate whimper.

During these final years at RKO the two sides of Mitchum

seem to have grown steadily apart. At home he was the lovingly anxious father, watching for the postman each day when his elder son Jim was visiting the folks back east. He started taking the boys out into the mountains on hunting and fishing trips after converting a Ford truck into a mobile camper. In March 1952 Dorothy gave birth to a third child, their first daughter, who was named Petrina after Mitchum's grandmother.

Away from home the period of relative quiescence which had followed the bust gave way to a series of fractious incidents. On location for *One Minute to Zero* in November 1951 he got into a fight in a Colorado Springs bar, apparently leaping in to defend his co-actor Charles McGraw. His opponent was one Bernard B. Reynolds, a professional heavyweight boxer with nineteen knock-outs and a world championship eliminator contest to his credit. Mitchum won, and Reynolds was carted off to hospital with a suspected fractured skull.

One witness claimed the actor kicked Reynolds in the head. He denied it. 'I grabbed him by the lapels. He kept yelling and swinging his arms about. I put my arms around his. He shook his right arm loose and swung at me. I ducked the punch and we fell to the floor. It was pure self-defence . . . If I hadn't decked him he'd have decked me—might have been real painful . . . An actor is always a target for the belligerent type of guy who thinks he's tough and movie-men are softies. I never start a fight, but I assure you I can always finish one if there's no way out. This one was unavoidable and I'm sorry it happened.'

A year later Mitchum had some trouble getting an outside line on his dressing-room phone, and comprehensively lost his temper. According to the *Los Angeles Herald-Express*: 'Robert definitely made a partial wreck out of the room. He is said to have jerked two phones from the wall, to have broken a glass on his neon-lighted dressing-table and to have kicked a big ceramic pot holding a plant. After that he proceeded to the set and is said to have told his assembled fellow-workers, "If they treat me like an animal, I'll behave like an animal."'

Well, two phones, one light and one potted plant hardly qualifies as vandalism on a grand scale, but one is left wondering what he was so angry about. On returning from Africa a few weeks earlier he'd apparently let himself go rather, indulging in what Tomkies calls 'boisterous-style nights out with the boys'. This probably hadn't done much for his family's peace of mind, and indeed, soon after the dressing-room incident, he and Dorothy experienced a brief separation. The suspicion persists that an angry Mitchum is more likely to be angry with himself than with anyone else. Having chosen to live two distinct lives rather than one, and usually with great success, he seems to have found it difficult to cope when they presented him with conflicting demands.

The next 'sensational' news item concerned Mitchum and Palance in a Mexican bar, an outraged Mexican general with a gun, tables hurled, and a swift escape by the two actors. Mitchum's and Palance's versions of the story differed, but it all seems to have been a well-oiled misunderstanding. Either way, Mitchum's reputation as a troublemaker went up or down a notch, depending on the point of view.

The fact that he was making almost universally bad movies must have played a part in his occasionally explosive behaviour, and it must have been with considerable relief that he approached the end of his indenture to RKO. It had taken him until 1951 to pay back the legal expenses incurred in 1948–9, but after forming his own production company he was more or less assured of a large and steady income. He felt quite able to either turn down or walk out of Hughes' last few offers of work—*The French Line, Cattle Queen of Montana* and *Susan Slept Here*. All three proved thoroughly forgettable. In any case, RKO itself was now a fast-sinking ship, with losses in 1952 that matched the profits of 1946. Mitchum wanted out, wanted his independence, wanted—though he refused to say it explicitly—to make better films. RKO had made him a star, and it was doubtful whether even RKO could now turn him into a nobody, but Hughes' world was vanishing, as Hughes himself would eventually do, and it was time for Mitchum to adjust his career accordingly.

6 The Country Privy

Second Chance, 1953

'The Rin Tin Tin method is good enough for me. That dog never worried about motivation or concepts and all that junk.'

(Mitchum, 1968)

MOST MOVIE-GOERS didn't give a damn which company Mitchum worked for. They didn't go to see the wares of a particular studio, they went to watch their favourites going through their paces. They wanted more of the same rather than innovation—a new story of course, but a similar character fighting his way through it. Mitchum's own popularity, as he rightly observed, had not been built up by displays of versatility.

Who was this 'Mitchum character' that audiences enjoyed going to see in 1953? He was harder to categorise than most of the other leading men of his generation, a more complex mixture of virtues and vices than a James Stewart, a John Wayne,

With Marilyn Monroe in *River of No Return*, 1954

a Gary Cooper. The roles he played were not unusual—in the twenty-four films made since signing with RKO he had played six soldiers, five cowboys, three doctors, one private eye, one policeman and eight assorted romantic heroes—but his variations on them frequently were. His record with women was certainly untypical. He had emerged from only thirteen movies with the heroine in tow, and on no fewer than five occasions his leading lady had tried to kill him. Three had succeeded. It was hard to imagine any of James Stewart's heroines planning his murder, let alone five. Mitchum obviously had something which women found intensely resistible.

One attribute he nearly always lacked was class or, in American terms, money. A rich Mitchum character seemed almost a contradiction in terms, and when he wasn't playing the staple genre figures his occupations were anything but glamorous—an ex-boxer, an ambulance driver, a toy salesman. When a reporter asked him what he was playing in *Macao*, he answered: 'Need you ask?—a derelict adventurer'. He was only allowed into the middle-class realm to play doctors, and in each case this profession was little more than a plot device.

So the Mitchum character was an ordinary enough guy occupationally, and his level of intelligence usually reflected this ordinariness. He was no genius. His two most obvious attributes were physical toughness and sex appeal, the very characteristics which had gotten him into movies in the first place, but in his case they had not been used as building blocks for the creation of a celluloid superman. Mitchum's sex appeal had not been broadened into a character who knew how to choose or deal with women. On the contrary, he usually picked the wrong one on whom to bestow his affections, and even when he struck lucky with the right girl there was rarely any suggestion that life's problems had thereby been solved. Mitchum romances didn't have an idyllic future written into them because Mitchum, as a romantic character, was far too real. He was sexy, he was usually kind, but he wasn't an idealised male.

When it came to the characters' attitudes, there were few that transcended particular films. An overall attitude to life, however, was fairly consistently displayed. The character was cynical but by no means bitter; he might distrust hope but he was far from immune to it. That hope was always personally-based, on himself or another character, it never amounted to moral or ideological baggage. Mitchum, unlike Wayne or Ste-

Track of the Cat, 1954

wart or Cooper, had no message for mankind. What was right was right because it seemed so at the time, not because it furthered the American dream, the pursuit of freedom or the salvation of the downtrodden. He was quite ready to help damsels in distress, even to the point of self-destruction, because he had a good heart, because loneliness was less fun, because she looked sexy. Holy grails, though, left him cold. What could there be worth fighting for? The character moved through a world in which survival was the most he could hope for, run by authorities who didn't give a damn, populated by men and women who usually turned out to be trouble.

But once he did get involved you knew he'd stay involved to the bitter end. Mitchum might walk as if he didn't care whether he reached his destination or not, but once in motion he was impossible to stop, partly because his curiosity had been aroused, partly because stopping required more effort than keeping going. The character's inertia factor was awesome.

In one respect he was the sixties twenty years ahead of its time: he was subversive because he didn't care about the things which society said he should care about. He had no materialistic drive, no grand ambitions, no reverence for the female sex. But in another respect he was the sixties antithesis: he had no idealism either. He had nothing against materialistic ambition, it just wasn't for him. He simply didn't think in a social way, didn't pretend to make judgements or care about those made by others. He was just there, trying to cope as best he could. Like ordinary people, and unlike most 'star characters', his worst enemy was clearly himself. He was nothing special, and that was what made him special as a Hollywood star.

In his next four movies Mitchum began to break away from his character-image. Aspects of it remained of course, but suddenly the essential indifference of the persona was gone: here were four men, in four very different films, driven by a heightened sense of purpose.

River of No Return was a transitional movie in his career. Set in the nineteenth-century American Northwest, it featured Mitchum as an ex-con with a young son set on building a new life as a farmer in the wilderness. While he's been in jail his son has been looked after by saloon singer Marilyn Monroe,

Not as a Stranger, 1955

115

and the film's narrative naturally conspires to push the two stars increasingly together. Mitchum at first seems his usual unheroic hero-self, tough and reasonably competent on the one hand, all too human on the other. He wins the adoration of the son he's virtually abandoned by being his positive self, and displays his remarkable inability to read other people by assaulting Monroe and getting suckered by her man-friend. But as the film progresses the positive side emerges totally triumphant, leaving behind the overwhelming impression of a responsible, caring and self-confident man. This character knows what he wants.

Track of the Cat represented a more dramatic departure, in terms of both film and character. It was as near an art-movie as anything Mitchum had made, a Eugene O'Neill-ish tale of a divided family snowed in by winter and menaced by a killer mountain lion. Mum is unloving, Dad an alcoholic, their daughter bitterly old-maidish. The three sons, in order of seniority, are other-worldly, arrogant and innocent. Mitchum played the second, as unsympathetic a role as he'd yet played.

He managed it well; indeed, the acting was excellent throughout, and the film's weakness could be laid at director William Wellman's door. 'For seven years,' he later recalled, 'I'd looked for a story that I could do—and this sounds silly— in black-and-white in colour . . . the result, photographically, was fantastic. Never have I seen such beauty, a naked kind of beauty.' *Track of the Cat* is certainly beautiful to look at, and the bickering family offer a suitably bleak picture of human relations, but nothing ties it all together; Wellman seems to have been unable to decide whether he was making a melodrama or an art-movie, and ended up with neither. Critics and public were equally unimpressed, and Mitchum's first foray into big-time villainy went largely unnoticed.

Not as a Stranger found him just as obsessed, just as unsympathetic, and just as marooned in an ill-considered project. He played a doctor all the way from starving student to his own practice, disdainful of medical orthodoxy and money-grubbing colleagues, and quite prepared to sacrifice wife and friends on the altar of his own idealism. Stanley Kramer, who produced and directed, had a reputation for making hard-hitting films which dealt with social issues, and the conflict between integrity and pragmatism in the medical profession is well reflected in the opening half-hour. But thereafter the movie crumbles under the weight of its 'human dimension'. Mitchum's character, as the standard-bearer for integrity, treats his new wife (acquired to pay his way through medical school) so shabbily that he becomes totally unsympathetic, destroying his own case and the film's message in the process.

He comes good at the end, but by then it's far too late: nobody gives a damn whether he lives or dies.

The incredibility of this character was, if not Mitchum's fault, the fault of whoever cast him. He never *seems* driven, though the whole story rests on the fact that he is. The affair he has with Gloria Grahame seems like something left over from *Macao*: it's the old Mitchum drifting into something because it looks interesting, not the dynamic young doctor drunk on medical destiny. Mitchum could get away with obsessive evil, as he was soon to show, but at this time in his career crusaders did not appear to lie within his range. It would be easy to say that he was too cynical a man, that the character was too far removed from his own experience, but it's possible that the opposite was the case. Mitchum, at this age, probably had all the cynic's latent desire to believe, and such a role may well have been too close for comfort.

His character in *The Night of the Hunter* was definitely far-removed; an itinerant preacher, fundamentalist to the point of psychopathy, who wanders the Midwest confronting and dispatching evil. Since he equates evil with sex and sex with women, he kills women. In the opening scenes we see the feet of his latest victim protruding from a door and the man himself at a striptease show, feeding his righteous anger. As the lady disrobes his fist disappears into his pocket, there is a click, and the blade of a flick-knife rips out through the cloth of his jacket.

Meanwhile another man is being taken away by the police on charges of robbery and murder. He has told his young son where the money is hidden, and inadvertently reveals that his family knows the loot's whereabouts to his cell-mate, a friendly priest who's been picked up for auto-theft. He's hanged, friendly priest Mitchum is released, and the next time we see him he's standing by the lamppost outside the family home, throwing a giant shadow on the children's bedroom wall. He gets into their mother's good graces, marries her, refuses to consummate the union—that side of marriage 'disgusts' him—and sets about worming the secret of the money's location out of her. When he discovers that she doesn't know it, he kills her. The children manage to escape down-river and eventually find sanctuary with a Victorian-style earth-mother. Mitchum, meanwhile, is doggedly following their trail.

The plot tells the story, but *The Night of the Hunter* is not a naturalistic narrative movie. It was the only movie Charles Laughton was ever to direct, and it remains to this day one of the most integrated symbolic films ever to emerge from Hollywood. Startling image follows startling image for an hour and a half, transforming a simple story into an epic contest

between the light and the dark, good and evil. Mitchum always seems to be appearing in silhouette or in pursuit of his menacing shadow; Lillian Gish, as the earth-mother, is like human apple pie. Some of the scenes—the wedding night, the wife's renunciation of sex in favour of God, her body gracefully waving with the weeds at the bottom of the river— are intensely dramatic; others, particularly the children's escape down-river through a world of rabbits and owls, have a stark poetry that is somehow both corny and highly moving.

Since Mitchum's character, like everything else, is relegated to symbolic status by the film's style, it might be thought that it presented little in the way of an acting challenge. In fact the opposite was true. This kind of role involved the pulling together of realism and abstractionism—the preacher had to be convincing as both a symbol and a person, without the two facets contradicting each other. That he achieved this brilliantly was a testimony to both his natural talent and his determination to succeed. Years later he would recall that he'd 'never felt a keener sense of trying to please a director'. He even admitted that the film was 'pretty good'.

While the Mitchum character was breaking new ground in movies the man himself continued to make the headlines in traditional style. For a man who had now made more than fifty films he was still remarkably young, in his late thirties, and his penchant for exploding the strains of stardom in spectacular escapades would show no sign of diminishing until the decade was almost spent. It was no longer all his fault: like a gunfighter in a fifties western he invited trouble merely by having a reputation for it. But sometimes it was.

In December 1953 an LA motorcycle cop stopped him for speeding. Mitchum allegedly remarked, 'You gotta witness, bud? Well, neither have I. See you in court', and then drove off. The cop gave chase, and the actor was eventually charged with evading arrest, obstructing an officer and speeding. He claimed 'a hundred people did the same thing every day', but admitted it had been a mistake. The judge fined him $200. The following year another motoring incident probably cost him rather more, when he allegedly ran his car into the back of someone else's pride and joy at an intersection. The aggrieved party sued for $50,000, but the matter was resolved out of court and the public eye.

Night of the Hunter, 1955

1954 was the year for Mitchum to run into things: in April he collided with a softer obstacle, bare-breasted Simone Silva, on the beach at Cannes. 'The photographers got down on their knees to plead with me to take the top off,' Simone said later, and being a trooper she had obliged them. Mitchum happened to be standing nearby, and she snuggled up close. Judging from the photographs which flashed around the world, his attempts to escape her embrace were somewhat half-hearted. 'I never saw her coming,' he said ingenuously, 'I had my back to the sea and I could either stay put or leap into the sea to get out of her way. I just didn't jump, that's all. At first I didn't realise what was going on. I was having a good time, but when I saw the photographic evidence afterwards I got quite mad.'

Nobody emerged from the incident too happy. Two photographers broke limbs in the scramble to capture the moment for posterity, Simone was ordered out of town, and Dorothy was hopping mad. 'How would you like a picture of your husband showing him with such a girl being printed all over the world?' she asked the assembled press corps. Mitchum was presumably chastened by her if not the experience.

Two months later he was fired from *Blood Alley*, his first post-*Night of the Hunter* movie, in circumstances that still remain a matter for dispute. According to William Wellman, he was brought in as director by John Wayne, whose company was producing the film, because both the incumbent director and Mitchum were proving difficult. Mitchum, Wellman said, 'was on dope, always walking about six inches off the ground. He punched a guy, one of the drivers, knocked him into the bay, damn near killed him.' Wellman then told his bosses that either he or Mitchum had to go. Mitchum went, and 'Wayne had to come up and take over because it was one of his projects.'

Mitchum denied that the 'victim' in question even got wet. 'It was just horseplay,' he said. He accepted his dismissal—'there are no hard feelings, we just didn't see eye to eye'—but hinted, at the time, that other, hidden considerations had played a part. Twenty years later he was prepared to be more specific: 'I think that Duke Wayne . . . was renegotiating his contract with Warner Brothers because of a recent tax law change. They agreed providing he did one more film on the old contract and Duke said "I don't have another." "We got that picture up at San Raphael." And Duke said, "No, Mitchum's doing that." "Was." That was the end of that.'

The same month the Mitchums were fined $25 for keeping an unruly dog. Four times in the previous year the city dog-catchers had found the beast wandering at large, and Dorothy's explanation—that the dog had learned to open their gate—was not well received by the judge. 'Has he learned to answer the telephone yet?' he asked.

More seriously Mitchum found himself the subject of a story in the gossip magazine *Confidential*. In it Charles Jordan described a party at Charles Laughton's home, at which Mitchum had allegedly stripped, covered himself with ketchup, and said, 'This is a masquerade party, isn't it? Well, I'm a hamburger.' At this point, according to Jordan, Laughton had thrown Mitchum and an unidentified female out.

Mitchum said there was no truth whatsoever in the story and sued the magazine for $1 million. He told the press that though most stars preferred to ignore such fabrications rather than land themselves in endless court battles he was determined to see the matter through. 'I think it's a case of fighting for your own good name ... . People are inclined to believe what they read in magazines. They say, "If it's printed, it must be true. And if it's not true, how come they are able to get away with it?" And that's the whole point. They should not be allowed to get away with it.' And in the end they didn't. The endless court battle ensued, and Mitchum never received any money, but enough of his colleagues followed his example to bankrupt *Confidential*.

Meantime, his sense of humour was getting him into more trouble. He arrived in Trinidad for the shooting of *Fire Down Below* and was greeted with the usual intellectual questions, like 'what do you have in your suitcase?' 'Two kilos of marijuana,' he replied, adding for good measure that he'd recently had a transfusion of Jewish blood, 'so I can stay even with those guys'. A diplomatic imbroglio ensued, with cast and crew besieged in their hotel. According to co-star Jack Lemmon 'the State Department got into the act and there was talk of throwing us off the island. Old Mitch couldn't understand what all the fuss was about. He said, "Don't these people have a sense of humour?"'

The sailors who precipitated the brawl in a Tobago hotel bar some weeks later didn't seem to have one either. Mitchum and his wife were peacefully enjoying a cup of coffee when one of three sailors joined them in conversation. A second member of the trio then came over, told the first to shut up, and reinforced this simple message by hitting him in the mouth. Mitchum expressed surprise at the attack. 'Suppose I hit you,' said the attacker, and did. Mitchum hit back, knocking his assailant through some glass doors. Enter the third sailor, who took rather longer to subdue. The first one then revived and attacked Mitchum as well. The police and naval police arrived to find the bar littered with broken furniture and unconscious

mariners. Mitchum went back to his coffee.

Why does the United States bother with marines when it has Mitchum? Diplomacy, perhaps, was not his strong point. He described Australia as 'the easiest country in the world to get into and the hardest to get out of', with an 'aggressive hospitality' and a culture that deified 'steak, eggs and beer'. He liked Europe, except for the noise, and praised the Swedes for the coldness of their baths: 'those people would even swim in a martini'. He found the Greeks especially easy to get to know: 'The first time they meet you they ask you how much money you have, do you have halitosis, where you are vaccinated and do you like them. You say you like them and they kiss you. They have moustaches.' Even the canine world was given cause to tremble by Mitchum-at-large. 'Don't you think all dogs should be shot?' he innocently asked a collector for the SPCA.

This picture of Mr Trouble With The Barbed Tongue must have caused some trepidation in the hearts of those people and animals who signed on to work with him. They needn't have worried. His ovine co-stars in *The Sundowners* received exemplary treatment: in the shearing scenes, according to director Zinneman, Mitchum 'almost wept for fear he would lacerate the animals' skins and that they would bleed to death'. Jack Lemmon, recovering from a misunderstanding with his sunlamp—he used it for thirty minutes at three inches instead of the other way round—was cheered by the arrival of a bouquet from Mitchum, multi-coloured condoms tastefully arranged in a setting of stink weeds. On a rather higher plane, the wardrobe girl on *Heaven Knows, Mr Allison* remembered one day when Deborah Kerr indicated to the actor that she'd hurt her feet on the rocky ground: 'He just kneeled down, unlaced her white sneakers, removed them and massaged her feet. It was lovely the way he did it. No show, no affection, just all feeling. Then he put her sneakers back on and said kind of brusquely, "Gotta keep you alive for the next scene."'

George Hamilton, whom Mitchum helped through *Home from the Hill*, told the story of a dinner party they both attended. 'They were very kind to us, gave us a great time, and Bob didn't know how to say thank you. Their little girl had hurt her arm on a swing at the back of the house, so next day Bob wrote a note to the child saying "I want to compliment you on your choice of parents. I think you did a marvellous job of choosing them. It was a very wise, intelligent

Foreign Intrigue, 1956

choice." I think that shows his humour, his intelligence, warmth and natural timidity—which I don't think people realise he has. He is one of the kindest, nicest men I've ever met.'

One could say that this consideration extended from the cast to the crew, but in reality it worked the other way around. Mitchum has usually seemed more at home with 'real working people', and stories of him standing up for them against directors and producers are legion. On at least one occasion he 'withdrew his labour' until a sacked crew member was reinstated, and the sound engineer on *Heaven Knows, Mr Allison* remarked that when two people were taken to hospital after accidents Mitchum was the only member of the cast to visit them. He seems to have always had an instinctive feeling for the underdog, whether it was an extra being bullied by a director or Simmons being bullied by Preminger.

This Mitchum never hit the headlines of course. As a new item 'kindness shown by Hollywood star' could hardly compete with punch-ups or Simone's naked ambition. For his part Mitchum was probably delighted that it didn't. Charles Laughton noted that the actor wouldn't thank anyone 'for destroying the image he's built up in his defence', and Mr Trouble was probably the price he had to pay for staying sane. For one thing it provided a 'manly' counterpoint to the business of being an actor, for another it allowed the existence of another 'Mitchum', one who made movies and got into the sort of scrapes movie stars got into. This public Mitchum was not him, though perhaps he occasionally caught sight of him in the mirror at home.

The movie business, Mitchum told Hedda Hopper in 1953, 'is like a country privy. When you get enough shit in there, especially in the summer and not in the winter when it's frozen, it topples over of its own strain. Shit is shit. Now they've got these trick glasses and you can see the pile from both sides . . . You know, when business is bad in Hollywood everyone starts fleeing in panic. During the depression the auto business was in a bad way. But what did they do? Instead of fleeing in panic they re-tooled, turned out completely new models.'

The moral was clear enough, and Mitchum now had the clout to do something about it, to help the new Hollywood models roll off the production line. He was free of RKO, a big enough star to sell films on his name alone, with his own production company. But did he have the will to go where beefcake had never gone before?

The obstacles were not negligible. The American film

industry was hardly famed for innovation, and the country as a whole was only beginning to emerge from the conformist mania of the McCarthy years. Technical innovation—'seeing the pile from both sides'—was not for Mitchum, and in the context of the period the new models could only really assume two basic forms, a move away from the traditional narrative structure or a move towards greater realism within the confines of the narrative structure. It can scarcely have escaped Mitchum's notice that *Not as a Stranger*, a dramatic slice of soap containing one of his least convincing performances, had proved a smash at the box office, whereas *Night of the Hunter*, an original film containing one of his most memorable characterisations, had disappeared down the financial plughole trailing its critical raves.

A move towards realism within traditional structures seemed the best bet, and the success of actors like Brando over the coming decade proved that such innovation could be more than financially viable. But Mitchum, for reasons that must relate back to his lack of ambition and drive rather than to any deficiency in intelligence or talent, chose to funk the opportunity. Seven of his next eight movies would be routine Hollywood: two more cowboys, three more soldiers, a spy, and the inevitable derelict adventurer.

Most of these films were unexceptional rather than bad. *Man with the Gun* (*The Troubleshooter* in UK) had a formula western plot, but still managed to reflect the changes the genre was going through. The hero was no saint, the dialogue sounded like it had been written rather than reshuffled, the town was suitably demoralised. *Foreign Intrigue*, which followed, was a TV spin-off best forgotten. Mitchum wandered around Europe in a trench coat, meeting a corpse, a suspicious widow and blackmail in Vienna, a love interest, another corpse and more blackmail in Stockholm, etc. The *New Yorker* thought he looked 'even more bored than usual'.

Bandido, which was Mitchum's first co-production, found him gun-running in Mexico. Richard Fleischer's direction caught the magnificence of the scenery and made the most of some vigorous action sequences, but the story was unoriginal and the musical score quite appalling. *Heaven Knows, Mr Allison* offered a profound change of pace, with Mitchum and Deborah Kerr playing the soldier and the nun marooned together on a Pacific island during World War II. There was a real opportunity here for director John Huston to create something interesting, but with the censors peering over his shoulder he opted for understatement, and ended up with no statement. Both Mitchum and Kerr are totally convincing, but the failure to explore the relationship between them gradually

125

reduces that relationship to a gimmick.

Heaven Knows, Mr Allison was the first of three movies Mitchum made in a deal with Twentieth Century-Fox, but before moving on to the other two he made *Fire Down Below* for Warners/Columbia. This was the derelict adventurer role, with Jack Lemmon cast as his sidekick and Rita Hayworth as Jane Russell. It was the old Hughes formula, two men and one woman in an exotic location (in this case the Caribbean), but nobody seemed to know how the formula was supposed to work. The first half of the film features the triangle, the second is all melodramatic action. Hayworth does her obligatory dance and encapsulates her life history in true formulaic style: 'I'm no good for you. No good for anyone. Armies have marched over me.' Lemmon licks his lips, Mitchum leers, the adolescents in the stalls drop their popcorn.

The other two Fox films were war dramas. *The Enemy Below* featured a gripping duel in mid-Atlantic between a destroyer and a U-boat, with Mitchum and Curt Jurgens as the respective captains. Neither is asked for very much in the way of acting, but no false notes are struck, and as conventional war movies go *The Enemy Below* is better than most. The climax, in which both ships are sunk and the two enemy crews help each other survive, is one of the simplest and most effective cinematic evocations of war's absurdity.

The Hunters was also directed by ex-actor Dick Powell, but there the comparisons ended. The aerial action in this Korean war story won almost universal praise, the rest of the movie almost universal condemnation. The characters are pure cardboard, the dialogue about as sensitive as Afrikaaner ideology. Mitchum, looking back on the film, resorted to a ploy that was to become increasingly familiar in the sixties—a jokey explanation of how he came to be caught up in such rubbish. Dick Powell, he told Roderick Mann, sent him thirty pages of the script, and 'it seemed fine to me. I got to fly a fighter plane and spend a lot of time in the Officers' Club in Japan. "And you can go to Japan early and scout it out for a couple of weeks," he said. That sounded good, so I said yes. Then he sent me Page 31. And I found out my plane crashed and I spent the rest of the film carrying some fellow through Japan on my back. "You ought to cast that part by the pound," I said. "Find some wisp. What's Sinatra doing?" But of course they saddled me with some hulk who got heavier by the minute and we did the whole thing on the Fox ranch.'

Heaven Knows, Mr Allison, 1957

126

Gullibility, however, hardly offered an adequate explanation of his relatively nondescript record in the fifties. Talking to Robert Robinson in 1958 he cast the net wider, blaming himself, 'them', and the system. The parts he liked, he said, were 'passive parts. I can't stand strenuous activity. Just mute passivity. People say I play myself in every part. I don't know. I just stand and do what I'm told. I point in the direction they tell me to. If they ask me what I think, I tell them and it only provokes arguments. So I don't like to be asked. I like to be told . . . I'm not really attached to acting, although I could have gotten attached if they hadn't forced me to go on making the same pictures over and over again. It isn't your fault if you make bad pictures—all that is required of you if you are a so-called film star is to stand there and register so much meat.'

This statement, half-serious and half tongue-in-cheek as usual, contains most of the contradictions which make Mitchum's career so fascinating. On the one hand, the question has to be asked—just who was forcing him to make the same pictures over and over again in the fifties? He could, for a while at least, have made virtually anything he wanted. On the other hand, he admits to indolence, yet applies it only to the acting side of the business, not to the choosing of the projects themselves. The reverse was much more the case. While he may well have drifted into particular movies out of sheer laziness, once on the set he remained the dedicated professional, anything but lazy.

The directors who worked with him during this period stumbled over each other in their rush to applaud his talents. John Huston thought him 'one of the finest actors I've ever had anything to do with . . . an actor of the calibre of Olivier, Burton and Brandon. . . He simply walks through most of his pictures with his eyes half open because that's all that's called for, but he is in fact capable of playing King Lear.'

Robert Parrish, who directed Mitchum in both *Fire Down Below* and *The Wonderful Country*, soon realised that the actor's apparent carelessness was a pose, that he always knew the lines he was pretending to learn at the last minute. Mitchum, Parrish said, 'will give a creative performance if he believes in what he's doing. If he doesn't, that's when he differs from other guys. They'll say, "We can't do this, it's terrible." But he just hits the marks. If you say, "Mitch, that's not very good," he'll say, "I'm paid to say it, not to write it."'

Richard Fleischer had a revealing experience with the actor. 'I was trying to get a close-up of him reacting to something and I said, "Action!" and nothing happened. So I cut and said, "You're supposed to react." "I did react." "Well, I didn't see it." And he said, "Well, it's the best I can do." I thought,

128

Jesus, he's pretty snotty. We run the dailies the next day and by God you look at the screen and he *is* reacting. It's on the screen and I couldn't see it.'

This remarkable talent offered a better reason for Mitchum's survival as a star than his own oft-quoted explanation, that if Rin Tin Tin could survive bad movies then so could any piece of meat. Another reason could be found in the fact that the Mitchum character established at RKO had, after the excursions of 1953-4, been re-established. He was a little less interesting perhaps, a bit straighter, less vulnerable, but he still made most of the current leading men look one-dimensional. Even in a pure 'man's film' like *The Enemy Below* he could offer a hint of something besides toughness, a sensitivity that was never sentimental, that complemented the toughness rather than ran against it. Unlike almost all his contemporaries, Mitchum didn't play the tough guy with men and the tender guy with women, he played both with both. He still seemed real, even when surrounded by mummery.

The two films that straddled the abysmal *The Hunters* provided vivid illustrations of the two Mitchums at work, the one who wanted to make 'new models' and the one who seemed quite happy adding to the pile in the country privy. *Thunder Road*, which he produced, wrote and starred in, would be by far his most personal film; *The Angry Hills* was just another piece of work, reviewed by Mitchum himself with the usual mix of mockery and self-mockery, complete with a tall tale explaining his involvement.

'Originally they wanted Alan Ladd for the part,' he said, 'but when they [the producers] got to his desert home to see him, he had just crawled out of his swimming pool and he was all shrunken like a dishwasher's hand . . . he was so small they could hardly see him, and they decided he wouldn't do for the big war correspondent . . . Some idiot said, "Ask Mitchum to play it. The bum will do anything if he's got five minutes free." Well, I had five minutes, so I did it.'

After reading the script he knew what he was in for. 'I play a mute war correspondent who gets to freeload on the Greek peasants,' he told Robert Robinson. 'He has trouble with goats. There are goats all over the place in Greece and this war correspondent, he's fighting it out among the goats and the heat. I don't know if he's a hero or a villain. I'll be clearer on that when the writer gets back.'

In other words he didn't give a toss what the story was. It was going to be the usual rubbish, and he was quite prepared to hit his marks. The director, Robert Aldrich, was obviously

not so wise in the ways of the cinematic world. 'We're making a lousy movie,' he told Mitchum. 'I'm trying the best I can, and I sense you are, but it's not working and I don't know what to do.' Mitchum told him they were making a 'gorilla picture'. Aldrich looked blank, so he defined the term: 'a gorilla picture is when you get $250,000 for doing all the wrong things for ten reels and in the last shot you get the girl and fade into the sunset. That's a gorilla picture. I don't care how well you make it, it's still going to be a gorilla picture. Now, if you understand that, you'll be very happy. If you don't, you'll be very unhappy.'

So much for *The Angry Hills*, alive to the sound of clichés. *Thunder Road* is not a gorilla picture, though at first sight it looks suspiciously like one. Mitchum plays Luke Doolin, the elder son of an Appalachian family which supplements its meagre income in the time-honoured way, by making and selling illegal liquor. The Doolins and the other local families involved in this trade have two enemies to worry about: the US Treasury Department, represented by 'T-Man' Troy Barrett (Gene Barry), and the big city crime syndicate headed by Carl Kogan (Jacques Aubuchon), which is determined to wrest control of the lucrative business from the country-folk. The place of confrontation is the road, with both the Feds and the gangsters out to intercept Luke and his fellow drivers as they ferry the liquor from the hills to the cities.

One man is killed, and the locals discuss and finally reject Kogan's offer to buy out their independence. Luke is the key figure, a fact which Kogan soon realises. The two meet, but when Kogan starts threatening Luke's family Luke simply judo chops him, leaps from the window, into his car and drives away. Meantime, the Feds are closing in on both Kogan and Luke. The former is arrested, the latter tries one run too many, ramming his car into a high-voltage sub-station.

On the surface then, *Thunder Road* is a straightforward thriller, and not a very convincing one at that. It has no sparkling dialogue, no deep characterisation, interior sets which RKO would have been proud of, and a plot which solves its own confusion by killing its conventional anti-hero in a blaze of anti-glory.

Beneath its cut-price surface, between the lines of its plot, *Thunder Road* also tells another story. Luke Doolin has been away in the Army, he's seen the world, and though he's now back in the family nest he knows that things will never be the

Thunder Road, 1958

same again. His love for his family, his respect for the local community and its traditions, are now part of a wider horizon; he no longer knows where 'home' is. His night-club-singer girlfriend (Keely Smith), geographically placed at the city end of the whisky run, also represents the other psychological pole of his existence. She and the family are like two magnets pulling him to and fro along the road, which becomes his only home, a metaphor for both freedom and limbo, positive and negative.

This split in Luke is exteriorised by the film into the world it portrays. Though the values of the local community are seen as superior to, as more human than, the values of the Federal and criminal bureaucracies, it is clearly recognised that the traditional way of life is doomed. Luke's younger brother Robin (played by Mitchum's son James) has great mechanical aptitude, and Luke is determined that he should qualify for the new world, for the future, as an engineer. He mustn't be allowed to share, as he wants, the freedom/limbo of Luke's road. In the end it is Luke's insistence on saving his brother that leads him to his death, the past sacrificed on the altar of an inferior future. *Thunder Road* is pervaded by melancholy.

And the split in Luke is also, in a way, the split in Mitchum. His magnets have always been the Hollywood tradition and the family tradition at one end, nonconformism, his love of literature and writing at the other. He has never felt completely at ease with either, and like Luke Doolin he's simply kept on going, moving from one pole to the other without ever really arriving, because he could not make the choice. Making movies has been Mitchum's 'Thunder Road'.

In 1959 the Mitchums moved out of Hollywood and into a farm they had bought on the other side of the country, on the Delaware shore of Chesapeake Bay. They had been contemplating such a move for several years, and for several reasons, of which their children's welfare was probably the most important. Mitchum, by all accounts, was a caring and conscientious father, but there wasn't much he could do about being Robert Mitchum. When the *Confidential* affair had broken in the press, his younger son Chris had been asked to leave his school and his daughter Trina had been forbidden to play with a friend by the friend's mother. Mitchum knew the woman: 'she was having an affair with a producer friend of

Robert Mitchum turns calypso singer, making his first record in 1958 for Capitol Records

133

mine whose wife was her best friend. Real nice.' But there was nothing he could do about any of it; Hollywood was Hollywood.

On a later occasion his elder son introduced Mitchum to one of his friends and later told his father that the friend no longer envied him his famous dad. 'How can you follow an act like that,' the friend had said. Jim was trying to get into movies too, and having dad around was likely to be more of a hindrance than a help. A move back East might help all the children.

Dorothy had long wanted to return, having always preferred the East coast to Hollywood, and Mitchum seems to have been eventually persuaded that he could do so without damaging his career. More and more movies were taking him abroad in any case, and a move would offer some useful advantages. He'd get back some of the privacy he'd sacrificed for stardom, and there would probably be less people in rural Delaware itching to hit him with a convenient bar-stool. Perhaps in the back of his mind it also made sense to split his life geographically, as it had already been split by his personality and his public status.

He was definitely mellowing as the fifties drew to a close and his own forties began. In August 1959 he made headlines by avoiding a brawl in Dublin, despite being subjected to the most extreme provocation. According to actor Richard Harris the assailant 'had three friends with him. He hit Mitchum full in the face when he wasn't looking. Mitchum could have killed him but he just shrugged it off like he does in film fights. He was wonderful.'

Perhaps it was age, perhaps it was growing wisdom. 'Let's face it,' he said, 'the most endearing thing about stardom and life and experience is that I've been able to improve.' Watching the development of his son Jim—'nine foot tall, beautiful, and every chance in the world to be an ass'—was doubtless giving him pause for thought about his own life. It was a time for taking stock.

The three movies with which he signed off the decade all reflected, coincidentally or not, this thoughtfulness, with three characters who seemed to reflect different sides of Mitchum the person. *The Wonderful Country* was a western, his best since *Pursued*. He played a derelict adventurer for a change, caught up in a plethora of conflicts involving Mexican bandits, Apaches, Texas Rangers, the US Army and railroad barons. But this adventurer is much more than a mobile cynic, and the grandeur of the 'wonderful country' seems to find an echo in his struggle for survival. The extreme individualism of the Mitchum character, and the problems it tends to create for him, have rarely been better portrayed.

Home from the Hill was the weakest film of the three, a modern Texas melodrama which today looks like a trailer for *Dallas*, with Mitchum as the proto-Jock, Eleanor Parker the suffering proto-Ellie, George Hamilton as proto-Bobby and George Peppard as a composite proto-JR/proto-Ray. People get pregnant but don't let on, people discover that their father isn't their father, people get shot. It's Texas, folks, where men have to be men and the women have to put up with them.

Despite this (now familiar) hodge-podge of reality and wishful mythologising, the acting, particularly from Mitchum and Parker, is more convincing than the makers of *Dallas* could imagine. Mitchum, as the lecherous old patriarch strong on the masculine virtues yet vaguely aware of their cost both to himself and his family, is painfully watchable.

It would be impudent to suggest that Paddy Carmody, the central male figure of *The Sundowners*, is the closest that Mitchum has come to playing himself, but the parallels between the character and the man are certainly there. Carmody is an itinerant sheep-drover, who travels back and forth across the Australian Outback with his wife and son. He loves living on the road, knowing that he's not tied down, and the backbone of the film is the conflict between this love and the equally strong love he has for his family. His wife (Deborah Kerr) wants to settle down, have a proper home, and their son shares her desire. Husband and wife cover their disagreements in jokey banter and survive them because of the strength of their mutual love. Paddy may be selfish, irresponsible, a little boy sometimes, but he's also a very caring man. His wife is a mixture of determination and passivity. They're a real couple, living on the delicate line between self-abnegation and other-abnegation, and all the film's best moments come from the exploration of their relationship.

As a film *The Sundowners* is far too long, far too travelogue-ish, and far too full of Peter Ustinov, but as a piece of Mitchum's career it is virtually priceless. Perhaps he too felt that Paddy Carmody offered a definitive portrait of his own contradictory character. It would be ten years before he acted so close to home again.

Overleaf: With Deborah Kerr in *The Sundowners*, 1960

7 Me Tarzan, You Gorilla

The Wonderful Country, 1959

'Why don't we quit and try something else. Like another movie.'

(Mitchum on the set of *The Good Guys and the Bad Guys*)

THE MARYLAND farm provided a pleasant retreat both from Hollywood life and making movies abroad. 'When I'm there,' Mitchum told Susan Barnes in 1960, 'I can sit around and watch the weeds grow. I have a boat, so if there's any work to be done I can hop on it and disappear . . . and hell!, the countryside is so flat you can see anyone coming. Slam the door. Hide. Get out the shotgun. Turn loose the dogs . . . If a car gets through the gate the dog won't let the people out of the car. After a while they get bored and go away, or die of carbon monoxide.'

He claimed he'd only known such delightful privacy in jail, or in driving alone across the continent. Then he'd been prone

The Last Time I Saw Archie, 1961

141

to stop at a convenient stretch of water and take out his rod. 'Fishing,' he thought, was 'man's ancient and honourable excuse for doing nothing.' It allowed him to meditate, to day-dream. On the farm he never lacked the opportunity to just turn off.

This mellower Mitchum was no invention of the publicists. The regular headlines of the fifties were not to be repeated in the sixties; Mitchum, in his own words, had 'learned to relax with just a few people—my wife, my children, a handful of friends. And I hope that, in their books, I'm a good guy with faults they can bear. If they can stand me, that's the most any-one deserves.' His marriage seemed as enduring as ever, and seemed to be gathering stability as it endured. He admitted that it had often been difficult for Dorothy, that sometimes she couldn't understand his hobo instincts, but he paid tribute to her 'adaptability'. For her part Dorothy noted that they'd been married since childhood, and that 'in a way we've had to learn about the world and each other and to grow up together during our marriage'. Asked how he'd cope without his wife, Mitchum replied: 'I don't think I could make it on my own now. Everything would wind up a compromise. Or I'd wind up in prison. I'm not safe to be let loose, you know.'

Towards the children he practised a 'loving indifference— that is, I treat them like I want to be treated—except, of course, when they ask for money. Then I give my best per-formance, one of my best, as a father from way back.' More seriously, he was determined to give them enough food, education and money to set them on their feet, and then let them choose whatever it was they wanted to do. The only thing he tried to impress on his two sons was that they could learn from his own experience. '"If you look real close at me," I said, "and look at the scars, you'll see that there's a hard way and an easy way." They listened to that I think. They *needn't* have it the hard way.'

When it came to money, Mitchum certainly had enough to keep the family in the style to which it was accustomed. And that, it seems, was enough. He griped about taxes like most Hollywood stars, but more in the manner of a *Thunder Road* moonshiner complaining about federal interference than of a man really concerned with amassing wealth. In fact it's hard to believe that money has ever been Mitchum's primary motiva-tion for doing anything. When he signed for *The List of Adrian Messenger* director John Huston suggested that he accept a painting, rather than cash, in payment. Back in the States the painting would be worth twice as much; he could then lend it to a museum and save the tax. 'Well, that may be all right,' Mitchum said, 'but it was much too complicated for me. I

142

took the money.' The conservation of time and effort were well worth an extra $75,000. He seems to have usually examined contracts for the number of days off before deigning to look at the fee.

He didn't mind making movies, but he did enjoy watching the weeds grow, and as the sixties began Mitchum seemed to be finding an increasing contentment with life away from the cameras. It was perhaps unfortunate that the decade of his growing personal content should turn out to be the decade of his country's discontent.

Mitchum had always denied being a bona fide rebel, claiming that he was 'so middle class it hurts'. Nevertheless, he had often appeared in an anti-establishment guise, both on and off the screen. Mitchum the character seemed more interested in sex than romance, Mitchum the character and Mitchum the man seemed consistently unimpressed by the great protestant ethic—work hard to get rich. So at one level the changes which rocked (but didn't roll) America in the mid-to-late sixties seemed promising territory for him. Sexual liberation was all over the place, avowed materialists hard to find.

At another level Mitchum proved as unimpressed by this brave new world as he had been by the brave old one. His attitudes remained fairly consistent, while society, or at least a large and vociferous section of its cinema-going population, swung past him towards the opposite extreme. Mitchum, long a thoughtful radical, suddenly found himself something of a thoughtful conservative.

His attitudes towards 'women' were illustrative. Asked if age worried him he quipped 'only in women', the sort of remark which even in the sixties sounded like the echo of a past generation. Living with the Masai tribe in East Africa during the filming of *Mr Moses* he was bowled over by the tribal women. 'One day there was this ceremony for which the women shaved their heads, greased themselves with fat, anointed themselves with cow urine, had their ears stretched down to here, had misshapen feet and wore rings to distort their legs—and then had a tooth knocked out as part of a ritual. Yet they were the most electrically feminine women—I mean you could *feel* it—that I'd ever come across . . . it's difficult to explain but there was something suppliant and at the same time compliant about their behaviour that got right under your guard.'

Suppliant? Compliant? Hardly words that feature in a feminist lexicon. Yet at the same time it's hard to imagine many male Hollywood stars, particularly of Mitchum's gen-

143

eration, who would even have noticed the Masai women's 'femininity'. He didn't think he was putting women down—they were just being their real and equal selves. 'They are equal all right,' he said on another occasion, 'but their role is a complementary one to man's. They have a different function in life both biologically and socially.' He admired women, didn't resent women with brains and ability, got on better with women than with men, but . . . 'real feminity' was 'a recognition by a woman of a man's role'.

His political views found Mitchum stranded in a similar no man's land. When asked about international affairs he said? 'Listen. I've read only one newspaper in three years. I figure if things get really tough they'll sound the siren.' But he felt concerned enough to visit Vietnam twice during the American occupation, and came back with some typically equivocal impressions. He found it 'quite humbling that there are still people of high purpose and straight direction'—he meant the ordinary soldiers, not the generals or the politicians—yet still defended the rights of those who refused to go. He could sound like a mad right-winger one moment, calling Jane Fonda 'a bigger threat to the Indians than gonorrhoea', and a radical the next: 'While the Dupont family has a whole wing of a Washington hospital reserved for them in case any one of them gets ill, humanity is facing a world crisis. Why the hell can't we get together?' He could also sound his usual cynical self: 'Politics is dishonest and you can't avoid it.'

He claimed to be a 'utopian anarchist', but agreed that meant 'nothing'. Being both anti-state and pro-underdog really put him in the paternalist camp, but if so the paternalism was undoubtedly benign. 'Just because I'm bigger than you and can maim you doesn't give me any right to bash your brains in,' he told Carrie Rickey in 1982. 'You don't get away with shit in this world and your only alternative is figuring out what you can give to others, not take from them.' It's easy to see how Vietnam must have given him doubts, as the paternalistic element in American policy clashed head-on with the reality of maiming.

Basically Mitchum was ill-equipped to deal with the sixties. Too enlightened to damn the new ideas out of hand, too intelligent and too set in his ways to damn all the old ideas, he remained where he had always been, and where he presumably felt most comfortable—on the fringe. The new generation's stress on the value of commitment simply passed him

Cape Fear, 1962

by, and after spending two generations on the fringe of the old mainstream culture he now found himself on the fringe of the new mainstream culture.

None of this would have mattered if he'd been just a simple Maryland farmer. People still needed to eat, food still had to be grown. He could have gone fishing in his spare time, meditated on it all, and reached his own private conclusions. As it was, he was a movie star, and his conclusions could not be private; even if he said nothing his movies would speak for him.

Hollywood was changing with the times. As TV mopped up the old mass market for escapist entertainment, the movies came to concentrate more and more on providing something special for its smaller, younger, and more discerning audience. This 'something special' took two basic forms: escapism which out-spectacled TV with more expensive effects, more explicit sex and bloodier violence, and a move away from escapism and into a more thoughtful, more realistic and more relevant storytelling. The old middle ground of light comedy, routine westerns and romantic soap opera was slowly squeezed out of existence.

This process occupied most of the decade, and for established stars like Mitchum it was still possible to make a living in the middle ground if they so chose. It was the easy option, and as such suited Mitchum, but it was also, in his case, something more: a statement of non-commitment, and of his own lack of faith in movies as anything other than escapist entertainment.

'Usually, you know, I make a film called *Pounded to Death by Gorillas*,' he told Jerry LeBlanc in 1968. 'They open up with a long shot of me standing and then a huge gorilla looms up behind me and hits me on top of the head. Boom, and I crumple. Boom, boom. I keep falling down and getting up again. Then they cut to a little girl skipping through fields of daisies and finally she comes to this house and a voice says, "Who's there?" As the writers haven't got that figured out yet, they cut back to me. Boom, boom, that gorilla is still knocking me down. And I'm still getting up again. Finally, the gorilla collapses on top of me, exhausted. Then the little girl comes in and says "He's around here some place, I just know." Finally, she peels away the gorilla and there lies our hero, me. So she hauls me to my feet, puts her arms around me, looks straight into the camera and says "I don't care what you think—I like him". So you know he's got to be a hell of a man . . . I've been playing it all my life. It's easier than writing you see. Every time the writers run out of words, they just kick the shit out of

146

Mitchum. A tried and true formula.'

This, then, was the essence of movie-making. 'To say you're in the business for artistic rewards is a sham. It's a nursery tale. I hate to repeat it, but the actor's original purpose was to keep the audience turned to the front while the pickpockets went to work from behind. I think, to some extent, that is still true.' The new 'slice of life' pictures consisted of 'an hour and seventy minutes about some guy's headache but they find a lot of empathy with the public. Guys say, "Gee, I know just how he felt."'

The new breed of stars got even shorter shrift. They might be good actors, but they'd 'been nowhere and seen nobody . . . these Method guys—they've done nothing. They *invent* experiences. I tell you, there's no substitute for the real thing. Today every fruit figures he's got to be an actor.' During the filming of *Home from the Hill* Mitchum was reportedly intensely irritated by George Peppard's 'method acting'; it must have galled him somewhat to see Peppard's performance singled out by several reviewers for praise.

As often with Mitchum's pronouncements, the aggressiveness was at least partly defensive. He knew as well as anyone that pure art and unadulterated rubbish were not the only alternatives open to film-makers. Had he made *Thunder Road* just for the pickpockets? The real choice was between movie-making as a job and movie-making as a vocation; the method actors' real crime was not their lack of experience but the fact that they took themselves and movies so seriously. Mitchum didn't want to take himself or his movies that seriously, and said so repeatedly, retreating behind his shield of self-mockery whenever anyone asked him awkward questions. His acting, he said, was 'even easier' than it looked. 'They don't pay you to invent in this business, just to follow the script and the formula.' So why was he so well-known for his professionalism? Ah, that was just 'a total lack of energy', he had learned to 'guard his enthusiasm'. It was the 'actual attendance' on-set that bothered him most: 'If you could just phone it in, *indicate* your attitude, I'd be happy. But I have to work because I have to write cheques. I have to cover my chagrin and embarrassment at not being born a Persian prince. I tell people I'm really born to the purple, but then they show up at the studio and see some assistant director saying, "come on you crumb". It's all pretty embarrassing.'

Mitchum made his living making movies—that was the bottom line. It was a job, and he didn't want to take it home with him. The type of films he usually made were chosen for that very reason: 'I can do them and walk away and just forget about them. It's all finished and I never have to see them. I

147

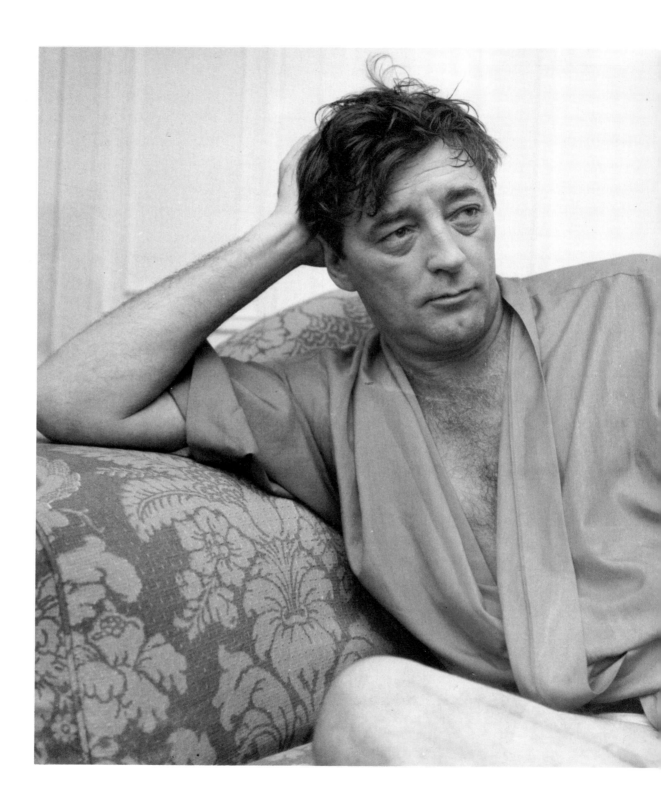

usually never do see them—and I'm not *involved*. Furthermore, I don't let anybody down. I don't want that responsibility. I don't *want* that deep involvement.'

Within those limits he'd do his considerable best. 'If you're trusted with the cash-box, you must bring some honest effort into it . . . If I'm to go through the general humiliations of the profession, I ought at least try to contribute something new and exciting if I can. I'm not sure how I do what I do. But anyone is welcome to try. I mean, the store is open to anyone to buy the materials Picasso uses.'

This approach worked well enough in the forties and fifties, with Mitchum contributing enough that was 'new and exciting'—and relevant—to make up for the large quality of formula fodder which he also turned out. It would work again in the seventies. But in the sixties such an approach would not, could not, serve him so well. Non-involvement condemned him to the shrinking middle ground, deserted by most of Hollywood's talented directors and spurned by its talented newcomers. Formula fodder would be all that was on offer.

Between *The Sundowners* and *Ryan's Daughter* he made nineteen films, and not one of them could be said to have advanced the art of cinema. Few of them were even entertaining, and Mitchum was increasingly driven back onto his last line of defence, explaining that his presence in the films was the result of either a mistake or a whim.

Thus, *The Night Fighters*: 'I was offered one script, but when I got to Ireland I was offered another. What was I to do—pay off all the actors and take a loss? Or do it?' Having disassociated himself from responsibility he felt free to compare watching the film with 'looking for a diamond that's been covered in sewage. You know it's there, but man does it smell!' When he did *The Grass is Greener*, an intended comedy, he excused himself on the grounds that he didn't have to 'grow a beard, fall off horses, or carry people round on my back', but when, several years later, he found himself in a string of routine action movies, he could be heard extolling the wonders of the outdoor life. 'They're not complicated and they're fun to make. Besides where else can you picnic under the trees?'

He made *Two for the Seesaw* because he admired Shirley MacLaine, *What a Way to Go!* because the producers wouldn't afford Sinatra, and *Rampage* because it came complete with a

Mitchum in a hotel room in London in 1963

family vacation to Hawaii. His qualification for *Secret Ceremony* seems to have been his renowned facility with accents. Not surprisingly he ended up on the set of *The Good Guys and the Bad Guys*, the nineteenth in this sorry run, exclaiming, 'How the hell did I get into this picture anyway? I kept reading in the papers that I was going to do it, but when they sent me the script I just tossed it on the heap with the rest of them. But somehow, one Monday morning, here I was. How the hell do these things happen to a man?'

How indeed? It was really no secret. Asked to name his favourite movie Mitchum would say *The Last Time I Saw Archie*. His reason?—'I got $400,000 for working four weeks and had a week off between Christmas and the New Year to go home to the farm.' It sometimes seems astonishing that he has managed to make any good movies at all.

Just 'attending', in the sixties, left him completely at the mercy of the producers, writers and directors. Nearly all of these nineteen films could have been made in the forties, and most of them looked and felt as dated as they were. Only one dealt with a serious social issue, and this was added as an afterthought. In *Secret Ceremony* he played an ageing satyr, and shared a bath with Mia Farrow to prove it. But when the film came out it was Elizabeth Taylor in the tub with Mia. As Mitchum explained, 'just after we shot *Secret Ceremony*, lesbianism came in . . . I'm no damned good as a lesbian.'

So much for art. Most of the film amply repaid Mitchum's lack of any deep involvement. *The Night Fighters* was a routine adventure which did less than justice to the complexities of the Irish situation, *The Longest Day* a routine war film of inordinate length whose claim to historical authenticity could best be judged by producer Zanuck's earnest wish that 'every time a door opens it would be a well-known personality'.

The Grass is Greener offered static drawing-room comedy in which all the money seemed to have been spent on the actors. Mitchum claimed, not for the first time, that he couldn't remember his lines, but fortunately there was 'a girl by the side of the set who told me when to say "Why?" or "Really?" when Cary Grant came to the end of a speech.' *The Last Time I Saw Archie* exchanged the drawing-room for the barracks, but the comedy, though less genteel, seemed just as static.

The List of Adrian Messenger, directed by John Huston, was a good murder mystery unnecessarily burdened by the gimmick of using disguised stars in cameo roles, Mitchum among

The Way West, 1967

151

them. *What a Way to Go!* had nothing but stars, *Rampage* was the sort of gorilla's gorilla picture which must have left its stars wishing they were in disguise.

The only three films of even average Mitchum quality from this period were *Man in the Middle*, a courtroom drama with a semblance of a serious theme, *Mister Moses*, an African adventure narrowly saved by Mitchum's lovably disreputable character, and *Cape Fear*, a straightforward shocker in which he pulled out every sadistic stop as an ex-con intent on making life unbearable for poor sweet Gregory Peck.

Between 1965 and 1969 he concentrated on westerns, interrupting a six-film sojourn in the sagebrush only for the aforementioned *Secret Ceremony* and a nondescript war movie, *Anzio*. The quality of the westerns was disappointing, particularly as at this time the genre itself was experiencing a rebirth. Films like *Hombre, Tell Them Willie Boy Is Here, Shenandoah, Will Penny, The Stalking Moon, The Wild Bunch*, Leone's 'Dollar Trilogy' and *Once Upon a Time in the West* were using the genre to reflect contemporary issues and sensibilities; America was examining itself in its favourite frontier mirror, and in the process producing westerns with a depth and relevance not seen for many years. Yet Mitchum's six had none of this: to most intents and purposes they could have been made in a time-warp.

Five Card Stud was a vehicle for Dean Martin's irresistibility, complete with two heroines fighting for his manly frame. Mitchum, as a diluted version of his *Night of the Hunter* preacher, hardly ever seems on-screen, and when he is it doesn't make much difference. Roddy McDowall, playing an adolescent J. R. Ewing, steals what there is of the picture to be stolen, and doubtless everyone but Dean Martin thought he was welcome to it.

Young Billy Young and *Villa Rides* were no better. The former was pure routine fodder, with Mitchum playing Robert Walker's father figure, Angie Dickinson's sleepy Lothario and the local villain's nemesis. *Villa Rides* had him playing Pancho Villa's entire air force in a film notable only for a witty performance by Charles Bronson (in pre-superstardom days), seemingly endless and unimaginatively filmed violence, and a script which seemed to belong to a different film. It was a gorilla picture *par excellence*; only the writers had not realised it. Mitchum, for once, really does look more than half-asleep.

The Good Guys and the Bad Guys at least seems aware of how

El Dorado, 1967

Overleaf: Ryan's Daughter, 1970

152

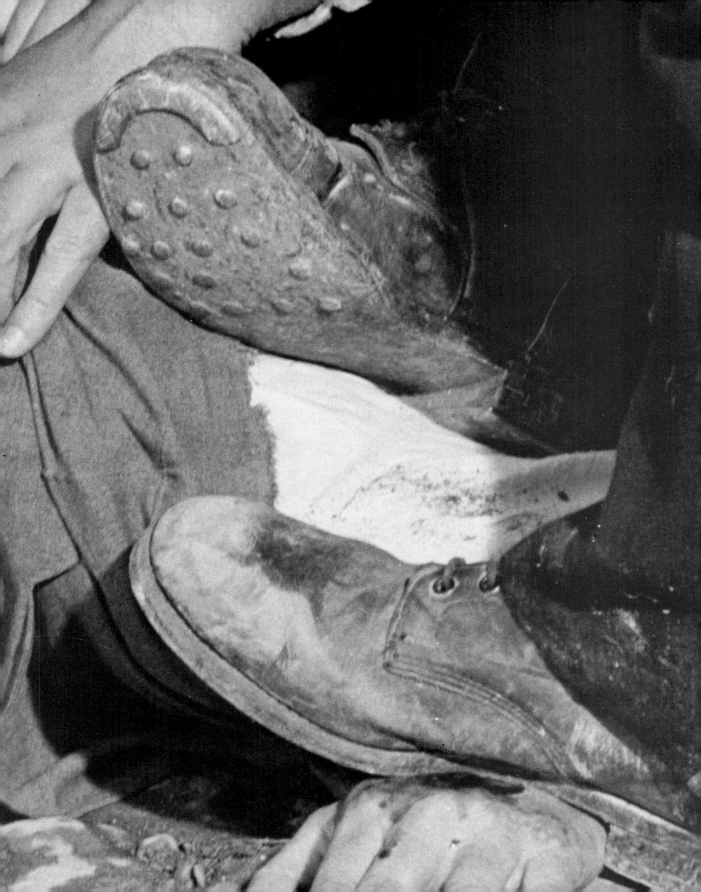

bad it is, sending itself up with some relish. 'Marshal Flagg, Marshal Flagg, beneath his shirt his shoulders sag' goes the persistent refrain, but it would take a worse script than this to sink Mitchum, who, like co-stars George Kennedy and Martin Balsam, seems to be having fun watching the clichés limp past. It all ends in a suitably silly chase. The name of the town—Progress—was presumably chosen on ironic grounds.

The remaining two westerns, though neither innovative or seasonable, were more substantial affairs. *El Dorado* was originally intended as a cinematisation of Harry Brown's novel *The Stars in their Courses*, but director Howard Hawks changed his mind in mid-project, incorporating a few scenes from the book into a re-make of his earlier classic *Rio Bravo*. The basic plot, the central relationships and many of the narrative set-pieces were transposed to the new film with only minor adjustments.

Unfortunately few of the updated scenes bear comparison with the originals. *Rio Bravo* has starkly drawn characters, and the beautifully staged set-pieces seem to flow naturally from them and their story; few films have such breathtaking clarity. *El Dorado*, by contrast, often seems something of a mess. The violence, though more extreme, seems less real. The humour is closer to farce, which further undercuts the sense of reality. There is little attempt made to establish character, and too often gimmickry is pushed into the subsequent breach. The lack of a strong female presence is particularly felt; in *Rio Bravo* the Angie Dickinson character lends depth to John Wayne's, and through him the relationship between the two principal men acquires a special resonance. The multi-dimensionality of the characters (by western standards) in turn provides the action sequences with an emotional power. *El Dorado*, lacking real characters, has humour and excitement, but no power to involve.

Seen from a different perspective, however, differences in intention between the two films emerge. In *Rio Bravo* the characters are all full of confidence in themselves, and curing Dude of alcoholism is merely a matter of restoring him to the confidence he has lost. In *El Dorado* there are continual references to age and failing powers, and these can be seen in the widest terms, as relating to Wayne and his image, to Hawks and his feelings about his own abilities, to the traditional Hollywood western itself. Just as Wayne needs trickery to overcome the enemy in *El Dorado*, so Hawks and Hollywood now need gimmickry to make the traditional western acceptable.

Mitchum doesn't really fit into this. His drunk, unlike Dean Martin's, has no psychological dimensions; his cure is accom-

156

plished physically, through Mississippi's evil concoction, not by appeals to his conscience and manhood. He is a very funny drunk, and the bathtub scene for which he was largely responsible remains one of *El Dorado*'s few improvements on the original, but he stands outside the film's basic flow. It is Wayne, clutching his side and hobbling down the street, who personalises the vanishing Hollywood frontier.

The Way West, though a lesser film, is more interesting from the point of view of Mitchum's career. As a film it should have been better; McLaglen, who'd first worked with the actor as Assistant Director on *Track of the Cat* and who'd recently made the excellent *Shenandoah*, had a fine novel to work from and a fine cast to work with, but somehow the parts never came together.

The plot concerns a wagon train's way west, with Kirk Douglas the obsessive-in-charge, Richard Widmark the leader of the common folk who grow to resent Douglas' over-demanding ways, and Mitchum the ageing scout who watches, through failing eyesight, as the wagons rumble into the land of soap opera. His is a moving performance, one that comes close to summing up his cinematic persona. He's an outsider, but not a loner in the more modern Clint Eastwood style. This latter character, at least in pre-*Josey Wales* films, is not so much an outsider as an alien; he has no real contact with ordinary people because such contact would set up a conflict between his hero-status and his humanity. If he's allowed to care he becomes vulnerable, if he doesn't he becomes inhuman, so he's not given the opportunity. Because he's so alienated from the rest of society, because his solitariness is so complete, the question of loneliness never arises. The Mitchum character on the other hand, in both *The Way West* and many other films, does meet ordinary people and does care. His solitariness is a function of his inability to share their dreams, and he knows that loneliness is the price that must be paid. He remains as divided as the Eastwood character is integrated, and that makes him both infinitely sad and infinitely real.

This character seems to sum up Mitchum's decade, stuck on the fringe of things, helping them along because they're there to be helped, yet devoid of any belief in a worthwhile destination.

Colour pictures: The Friends of Eddie Coyle, 1973; *Midway*, 1976; *The Enemy Below*, 1957; *River of No Return*, with Marilyn Monroe, 1954

157

8 Knight in Shabby Raincoat

The Friends of Eddie Coyle, 1973

Overleaf: Ryan's Daughter, 1970

'I didn't understand why they wanted me to play an Irish schoolteacher. Why not get a real Irish schoolteacher, I said. You can save my fare and he'll be a lot cheaper. But they took me.'

(Mitchum, 1970)

IN 1965 the Mitchums had returned to Hollywood, largely at Dorothy's insistence, and moved into a modest, ivy-covered mansion in Bel Air. Mitchum had also purchased a 76-acre ranch not too distant from LA, mostly as a home for his growing collection of quarter horses, and it was to the ranch that he returned late in 1968 after completing *The Good Guys and the Bad Guys*. He was tired, he told reporters, and hinted to several people that retirement was on the cards. Perhaps eighty-five movies was enough for one career.

Considering the quality of those movies he had graced over

Wrath of God, 1972

the previous eight years there was some reason for believing that the creative thrust of that career had run into the sand. Mitchum himself didn't seem worried by the lack of quality; indeed, sometimes he seemed to take a perverse delight in being associated with mediocrity, and there were few signs that he felt the urge to display his talents in more challenging circumstances. But he must have been bored with wearing the same hat in so many movies, in churning out professional performances in films that really didn't deserve them. Retirement would at least save him from having to choose between more of the same and more commitment.

As usual, however, there was another Mitchum to consider, the one who both enjoyed making, and saw some point in making, movies. A few years earlier he had seriously considered directing a particular project, only for the deal to fall through for reasons beyond his control. The man who had told Hedda Hopper that Hollywood needed re-tooling, who had worked so hard for Charles Laughton's original conception, was still there somewhere, hiding in the shadow of his other, more cynical self.

Both these Mitchums answered the call from Robert Bolt early in 1969. The first Mitchum had already read the script for *Ryan's Daughter* and greatly admired it. The second Mitchum had then pointed out just how long David Lean took to make a movie, and concluded that he couldn't keep himself 'glued together' for that length of time. After conferring, these two Mitchums reached their usual compromise—a wry joke. He couldn't make the film because he was contemplating suicide, he told Bolt. But for once he'd met his match. 'Well, if you'd just do this wretched little film of ours and *then* do yourself in,' Bolt promised, 'I'd be happy to stand the expenses of your burial.' Mitchum announced himself 'flattered, cajoled and seduced'. He would do *Ryan's Daughter*.

Or so the story goes. Big movies have big budgets and big stars in them get big fees. Mitchum's retirement fund would be nicely swollen, which would please Mitchum II. As for Mitchum I, it had been a long time since he'd been in a 'serious' film, made by people who were 'serious' about movies, surrounded by actors whose ability matched his own. The part was unlike anything he'd played before, an ageing Irish schoolteacher, gentle, kind, sexually inhibited. It was a challenge, and Mitchum I still relished challenges.

Arriving in Ireland Mitchum II took over. 'Until I got to Dingle my life was all downhill and shady,' he said. 'But this is now the most joyless period of my life—except for working at Lockheed and being in the army. I've put away more Scotch

164

since I got here than I've put away in my whole goddamned life . . . Ireland makes the rain a national monument, so the tourist scene lasts twelve months a year. After the first ten days of the film we were already seven days behind. So here I sit, practising my accent.'

It took the wardrobe department three months to fit him out. With a tight jacket he seemed to bulge; with a loose one, 'I just looked bulky, like a retired policeman . . . So it took them a million dollars and three months to get it right . . . in the end they had to pad up poor old Trevor Howard so as to make me look normal in proportion.' As for footwear, that was never satisfactorily resolved. 'I kept complaining about my feet but no one listened. David Lean told me to walk like a farmer, like a man used to trampling over loose soil. I couldn't do anything else, because my feet were killing me. If anyone praises that performance, they can put it down to some costume guy who couldn't find the right boots. I told them at the end of the picture that those boots must have been bought for Sarah Miles.'

As for the director's style, Mitchum II found it rather perfectionist. 'He shoots the film, then he re-shoots it. Then he looks at it all and shoots it again. The rehearsals take the budget.' A year later he remarked that 'they are probably still up there now, chasing some parasol down a beach, waiting for the wind to blow right and an old crew man to pull the strings correctly'.

While Mitchum II complained to the press Mitchum I was putting in his usual high level of effort. Trevor Howard noted how diligently Mitchum worked when he needed to, and John Mills recalled a particular incident which illustrated Mitchum's unselfish professionalism. 'With the strange half-animal character I was playing,' Mills said, 'it was sometimes difficult to hit crucial marks, and on one particular occasion, during the wild scene outside the pub on Rosie's wedding night, when Michael is being pushed and thrown around the circle of revellers, as I landed against Bob's shoulder I felt him unobtrusively turn me round until I was exactly in the right position for the camera to zoom in on a close-up.'

The film itself proved a disappointment. Like Lean's two previous films, *Lawrence of Arabia* and *Doctor Zhivago*, *Ryan's Daughter* took five years to make, but unlike them it lacked a story capable of matching the epic grandeur of its historical and physical settings. Trevor Howard was not exaggerating when he said that three hours was 'a bit long for a trifling love story'.

The caption at the beginning tells us that the year is 1916, the place Ireland, but the 'Troubles' in *Ryan's Daughter* are a

165

means of moving the plot forward, not of moving the characters. This is a love story, fairly pure and fairly simple. Rosie,
the village publican's daughter, reads cheap romances and
makes the mistake of thinking that marriage to Mitchum's
older schoolteacher will fulfil her fantasies. When he fails to
live up to her expectations she has a torrid affair with the shell-
shocked leader of the local British garrison. This becomes
public knowledge, and when the Brits intercept the national-
ists smuggling in German arms she is wrongfully blamed for
shopping them. The betrayed husband stands by her, but
can't stop the villagers depriving her of clothes and hair. The
lover, finding out she's gone back to the husband, blows himself up. The couple head for Dublin and a possible new life
together.

This story is worth about an hour; the film is more than
three hours long. For the remaining two Lean treats his audience to the wind making patterns in the sand, the clouds making patterns in the sky. The eye is feasted with seascapes,
fieldscapes, skyscapes, sunsets and a truly prodigious storm,
all of which seem much more fantastic than Rosie's fantasies.
All the actors seem dwarfed by the scenery, and on those few
occasions when they're allowed to fill the screen most of them
seem intent on making up for lost impact.

Mitchum had been miscast on purpose, Lean reasoning that
to have someone who is 'a simple, good man' play 'a simple,
good man' would be 'deadly boring'. This was an absurd
judgement: if the character was deadly boring in the first
place, then to cast Mitchum in the role would only serve to
undermine the credibility of both the character and the film.
Mitchum does a good job of effacing himself, but it is the audience that is left with the real chore of forgetting that his face
usually radiates cynicism rather than tormented goodness, and
it is given no help by Lean or the other males in the cast. It's
not just that there's nothing very gripping going on, there's
not even much that's convincing. Sarah Miles is fine as Rosie,
but her Brit lover is a twitching Adonis with a limp, the village
idiot is way over the top, and the villagers are strictly rent-a-
village (with a priest thrown in). Every now and then Lean/
Bolt throw a symbol at the audience to keep it awake—flying
seagulls for freedom, a stylus circling an expired gramophone
record for the marital rut, a jungle-like copse for passion.
Amidst all this sledge-hammer subtlety Mitchum's restraint,
through no fault of his own, comes to seem quite fantastic, and

With John Wayne in *El Dorado*, 1967

Ryan's Daughter ends up as little more than an audio-visual lesson in Irish meteorology.

While Mitchum had been spending his year in the Irish rain the rest of the world had been watching the sixties draw to an explosive close. Paris, Prague and Chicago were fast becoming folk-memories as De Gaulle, Brezhnev and Nixon made themselves comfortable once more in the seats of power. The Vietnam War went on as the peace placards rotted on sidewalks. Idealism turned inexorably into cynicism, and the movies reflected the transition.

Hollywood was going through a sea-change, as the last fragments of its old market for light entertainment were gobbled up by the TV companies. The new market was a young market, and the youth of the West wanted movies which reflected its preoccupations, not those of the preceding generation. The failure of idealism on a social scale led the movies in two basic directions, towards an escape from terrestrial reality in special-effect bonanzas like *Star Wars* and towards an examination of the American navel. The latter films were individual-centred, and centred moreover on individuals who knew that the social battles were unwinnable. They were anti-establishment because the new market was anti-establishment, but because the establishment was seen to be impregnable all their battles were with themselves. The old anti-heroes, the Brandos and Deans, had been anti-establishment heroes, but the new heroes were just that, anti-heroic. They were ordinary people trying to get along as best they could in the absence of ideals. The new stars like Nicholson and Redford were marked as people without illusions about society. Films like *Tell Them Willie Boy is Here* and *Five Easy Pieces* accepted Nixonism as an unfortunate fact of life; the trick was to come to some satisfactory compromise with an unsatisfactory world.

All of which sounded ready-made for Robert Mitchum, who'd been playing such characters before Korea, let alone Vietnam. The world of the early seventies, superficially more liberated, yet stripped of the ideological presentation he'd always found so offensive, must have made him feel quite at home. Both the squares and the liberals had been blown away.

Perhaps this explained the lull in intimations of his retirement. Perhaps it explains why he chose to make *Going Home*, an early seventies film *par excellence*, with its depiction of a world devoid of easy answers and its lauding of the so-recently derided virtues of compromise and 'live and let live'. Of course his stated reason for doing the film was more amusing, one more addition to the Mitchum collection of 'how-I-got-into-this-goddamned-movie' stories. 'At the same time as I was reading this script,' he told *The New York Times*, 'I was also reading a script about a jazz musician in San Francisco. So I ask myself, do I want to play a jazz musician in San Francisco, or do I want to go out on location in some godforsaken corner of McKeesport, Pennsylvania, and live in a motel for two months? No way. No way. So these two guys come in and we have a drink or two, and I sign the contract. On their way out, I say I'll see them in San Francisco. I thought they looked a little funny. Do you know what I did? I signed up for the wrong ———— movie!'

Well, maybe. He managed to turn down *Rio Lobo*—another, very tired remake of *Rio Bravo*—around this time, and if one is to believe all Mitchum's tales of how movies crept up on him from behind, one would be left with a picture of a benign idiot, tossed this way and that by the tides of chance. Mitchum is anything but an idiot, and it seems more than coincidence that whenever he stepped out of his deepening rut in the sixties and seventies his cover-story was about as convincing as a Reagan press conference.

Going Home is the story of a three-way relationship between father, son and the new woman in father's life. The twist is that father has just spent a long time in prison for killing his son's mother, and the son is not unnaturally somewhat confused emotionally. So confused, in fact, that he rapes the new woman, flees to the old family house and demands a meeting with his father there. He confesses to the rape, whereupon father beats him up. When the son demands to know why he killed his wife, father replies, 'Because I was drunk.' When the son asks what happens now, the answer is equally succinct: '*You* get to be twenty.'

It's a simple enough story, but the playing of Mitchum, Brenda Vaccaro and Jan-Michael Vincent make it eminently real. It's a film about getting through, about not being deflected by impossible ideals or useless regrets, and despite its lack of tension *Going Home* perfectly captures the spirit of the times. It might have been even better had the MGM president not chosen to lop twenty minutes off the director's final cut.

As if to make up for appearing in an 'involved' film Mitchum now chose to display his talents in one that was thoroughly silly. Director Ralph Nelson had recently made the headlines with the level of violence on display in his *Soldier Blue*, but in that film the subject-matter—the genocide of the native American population—at least provided some justification. *The Wrath of God* offered him no such excuse, but the bodies accumulated just the same. Mitchum, playing his third

gun-toting preacher, reportedly persuaded Rita Hayworth to make another comeback in this film, but it's difficult to understand why she agreed. She looks thoroughly bemused as the bodies and the crass symbolism pile up around her. The conclusion, with Mitchum lashed to a cross with barbed wire and managing to bring the whole thing down on top of his gibbering foe, provides an amusing climax to what was presumably intended as an unamusing movie.

The Friends of Eddie Coyle took Mitchum from the ridiculous back to the sublime. Another stereotypical early seventies film, it provided him with his most interesting role for a very long time, that of a thoroughly ordinary loser eking out a living on the margins of big city crime.

The story is set in Boston, where a team of highly efficient bank-robbers are pursuing their vocation. Being efficient they need a constant supply of untraceable guns, and Eddie Coyle (Mitchum) provides them. He in turn gets them from a young whizzkid (Steven Keats), who buys them, illicitly, from army personnel. The whizzkid is also getting some machine-guns for a couple of sixties refugees who have given up the peace movement in favour of grand larceny.

Eddie, meanwhile, has a problem. He's been convicted for ferrying stolen liquor, is coming up soon for sentence and an almost inevitable term in jail. The friendly fuzz (Richard Jordan) offers to help him avoid prison if he'll turn informer, and after some thought Eddie reluctantly helps with the capture of the whizzkid and his machine guns. This isn't enough for the fuzz, who now insist that he lead them to the bank-robbers. But by the time he's brought himself to do this they've already been shopped by his bartender friend (Peter Boyle). Even more to the point, the bartender friend has told the local syndicate that it was Eddie who did the shopping, and calmly accepted a syndicate contract for the termination of Eddie's life. This he carries through, and the film ends with the fuzz promising not to look too closely into the circumstances of Eddie's demise.

Cynicism pervades the film. Subtract the hopes of the sixties from the fears of the sixties and what remains is an all-embracing corruption. Neither the police nor the criminals have any fun; they are far too busy seeking promotion and/or wealth. Neither has any values, any morality save success. Eddie's a part of this world too, and he shares its pristine functionalism—one keeps one's word because one's knuckles get multiplied if one doesn't—but he's also old-fashioned enough

The Yakuza, 1975

171

to believe that friends are more than allies of convenience, and that fair play still retains some truncated meaning. Everyone else in the movie betrays anyone else without the slightest compunction.

Eddie is only on-screen for about 30 per cent of the film, but in that forty minutes or so Mitchum etches a rare portrait of the jobman criminal struggling to make life's ends meet. Age is getting to him, he's not too bright, and this new world of young whizzkids with no inhibitions is thoroughly unsettling. Yet he still knows how to enjoy himself, and the scene near the end where he relishes the simple joys of drink and a hockey-match only serve to demonstrate his humanity in a world which seems increasingly devoid of it. Throughout the story his dignity is somewhat precarious, and by the end it is in tatters as he pleads with the policeman for help in avoiding the jail term which will separate him from his family. Mitchum had never before played such a pathetically desperate character, and rarely had he acted with such conviction. For anyone who still doubts his talent as an actor, *Eddie Coyle* is the film to see.

The film unfortunately has eighty minutes without him. Yates' camera lingers over each bank robbery as if he's painting a masterpiece, but with no character development there's no tension, and the interior décor of suburban banks doesn't offer much interest to the eye. Furtive meetings between the various characters take up the rest of the time, and though we learn a lot about guns we don't learn much about the people discussing them. The emptiness of the dialogue is perhaps supposed to reflect empty lives, but no lives are that empty. The film might reflect a prevailing mood, but it does nothing to investigate or explain it. Mitchum's portrayal deserved a better frame.

'There's more than mere looks to Robert Mitchum's performance as Eddie Coyle,' wrote the *Times* reviewer. 'Now, at last, Mitchum achieves a kind of apotheosis . . . Self-consciously, with an old pro's quiet skills, Mitchum explores all of Coyle's contradictory facets. At 56, when many of his contemporaries are hiding out behind the remnants of their youthful images, he has summoned up the skills, the courage to demonstrate a remarkable range of talents.'

Mitchum, in grave danger of being taken seriously once more, hit back. He was only an actor because he couldn't think of any other job which paid as well; movie stardom had nothing to do with acting talent, as dear old Rin Tin Tin had proved. As for Eddie Coyle: 'When I was getting ready for the picture, I went to the barber to get an Eddie Coyle sort of hair-cut. I told him to cut it short but not too short. If someone says I give a good performance, you just tell them it's the haircut.'

Nobody believed him. He was a star, so he had to be special. A teacher of blind children wrote to tell him that 'my pupils believe that when you say something on the screen, whatever it is, it must be true. Your voice has the ring of honesty and sincerity in it.' A man sitting next to him on a plane calmly revealed that he and his wife had been discussing Mitchum only the night before. A woman rang up from a call-box on the other side of America to beg for his help. 'Please, you've got to come to Ohio to save my marriage,' she said. 'Every time my husband and I make love, I can't come unless I say your name.'

'Stuff like that', Mitchum admitted, scared the hell out of him. But what could he do about it? His disclaimers were now part of his legend—he was the movie star clever enough to know that movie stardom was a matter of luck and that movies were a matter of peripheral importance. People respected him more each time he told them there was nothing much to respect, which only made him search for more outrageous statements of his own unimportance. It was a no-win situation.

He could, however, still confound the critics by appearing in films lacking any distinction. He told the press that *Rosebud*, his next project, was 'little better than a comic strip', but he was making it anyway. It got him out of the house, 'otherwise Dorothy has me moving the furniture around'.

He wasn't away from home long. The director was Otto Preminger, whom Mitchum had worked with two decades earlier on *Angel Face* and *River of No Return*, and the two men quickly struck up a misunderstanding. 'One day the script had me looking beat-up and dishevelled,' Mitchum said, 'so I arrived on the set unshaven. "You are drunk", Otto roared, "and you cannot play this scene!" I argued with Otto saying how could I possibly be drunk at 5.30 in the morning, and pointed out the instructions in the script, but he wouldn't listen. "You are drunk and you are through!" he shouted. So I turned and yelled "Taxi!" and that was that.'

In 1975 Mitchum talked about the incident in his usual comic style, mentioning Preminger's 'triumphant history of mad behaviour' and regretting his dismissal on the grounds that 'Corsica's a nice place'. Four years later he called the whole business 'very sad . . . I regretted it later, as I'm sure Otto did . . . It really did break my heart.'

So, back to furniture moving and his other domestic pursuits. Even at home he couldn't escape being stared at, by his horse Don Guerro. 'I keep hitting him to make him stop,' Mitchum said. '"Remember you're just a horse," I tell him. "And that's all you'll ever be."' Don Guerro's reply is not on record.

Booze was one subject Mitchum did take seriously, at least some of the time. When Chris Petit and Chris Wicking interviewed him for *Time Out* in 1977 they received monosyllabic replies to nearly all the questions about movies—for example, Q: 'Were there directors you preferred to others?' A: 'Not really'—but an innocent question on preferred alcoholic beverages earned them around 500 words on the joys of Irish moonshine, fruit alcohol, mescal, pulque and other exotic brews and distillations. At other times he was less erudite, claiming variously that he drank as 'a preparation for death' and as a way of getting rid of people through out-drinking them. 'It takes thirty-six hours or more sometimes, and it nearly kills me. But in the end they go.' He did feel seriously enough about the dangers of booze to narrate the 1973 TV documentary *America on the Rocks*, which had been financed by the National Institute for Alcohol Abuse and Alcoholism.

In fact, in the seventies he seemed more prepared than before to speak seriously on some subjects. He lamented the glorification of trivia in the modern media, noting how those who had grown up in the shadow of television found it 'hard to be truly individual'. There was 'a group of people in their twenties to whom any marked significant breakthrough was meaningless, just like the next chapter in a television show'. The communications revolution offered hope for the future, but for the moment all it had produced was an 'advanced peasantry'.

What was needed was constant pressure for a greater individual awareness of what was 'really going on, for education and communication of the fine proved values and the true facts. It's the only hope really for ignorance leads to prejudice on all levels.' He believed that the Vietnam War, for all its sins, had provided 'some recognition of the need for communication'. He welcomed Watergate—'it's time people learned how the world is run'. He believed that 'everyone in the world should have at least the privilege of knowing what's happening all at the same time. One thing I've learned is that the greatest fuckin' slavery is ignorance, and the biggest commodity is ignorance—the dissemination of ignorance, the sale

With Jack O'Halloran (*left*) in *Farewell, My Lovely*, 1975

174

and burgeoning market of ignorance.'

He didn't expect dramatic progress. He hadn't bothered to vote in 1972, not believing that it made much difference 'who has his duke in the till . . . life is life, you know, so the new leader of Bangladesh goes to London to have his gall bladder removed and takes over a whole floor at Claridge's, and has an entourage of 200 people—two private jets he flies on. His attitude is fuck those starvers. *Fuck those starvers* . . . Well, what you do about it is *do* something about it. You put one brick on top of another—make it better.'

What the world needed now above all was 'good teachers and good writers', not, apparently, good movies. To Mitchum the movie world was a world apart. 'It's a dull, aching euphoria,' he said, 'there's all this asinine waste of money . . . This whole place has no relation to real life, real people. Oh, there are real people here, but they're in oil refineries and factories, not in movieland. This is Atlantis.'

In one sense yes, in another no. Movies were a part of the trivia he complained of, yet they were also possessed of an enormous latent potential for the spreading of truth and awareness. Mitchum, to my knowledge, has never explained why film is a less suitable medium than literature for the lessening of ignorance. Why has he not written for the screen since *Thunder Road*? Why has he not tried his hand at directing, as so many of his contemporaries have done?

Perhaps a lifetime in movies, carrying the bizarre weight of a public image, has bred contempt out of familiarity. After all, when you're worshipped merely for being present on a large screen in a dark hall, it must be difficult to take either yourself, the worshippers or the screen seriously.

The next film, *The Yakuza*, was a fascinating hybrid, featuring Mitchum as half-retired private eye Harry Kilmer let loose among the whirling swords of the Japanese underworld. He's been hired by Tanner (Brian Keith), an old wartime buddy, to clear up an apparent misunderstanding between Tanner and his Japanese, Mafia-style 'business partners'. Kilmer gets to Japan, where he'd been stationed during the occupation, and revisits the doomed love of his life (Kishi Keiko). She persuades her 'brother' (Takakura Ken) to help Kilmer sort out the problem. The 'brother'—unknown to Kilmer he's her husband—is a master swordsman who feels indebted to Kil-

Farewell, My Lovely, 1975

Overleaf: The Yakuza, 1975

176

mer for 'looking after' his wife during the occupation, so he agrees to help. His sword and Mitchum's gun finally triumph over the massed ranks of tattooed gangsters.

The plot often seems incomprehensible—according to Mitchum the final cut was cut once more—but the interplay of loyalties and cultures is clear enough. The emphasis is on America and its values; for the most part Japan is used as a killing-ground and a mirror.

Paulene Kael, the much-respected American critic, took exception to *The Yakuza*, suggesting that an ideogram for horse manure would be highly appropriate. The main thrust of her critique concerned what she saw as a glorification of violence; the success of *The Godfather*, she believed, had encouraged the film's makers to cash in on a spurious association of old world criminals and old world values. In doing so they had gotten the best of two nasty worlds, lots of violence and lots of self-righteous moralising.

There is some substance in this, but it is rather undermined by the practical implications of her other assertion, that director Sydney Pollack didn't really know what he was doing. Because *The Yakuza* has such a weak narrative thread attention is focused on Kilmer's character, and he, as an American sympathetic to, but forever distanced from, the Japanese way of life, carries the film's questions around with him. When, at the end, he slices off his little finger as a gesture of penitence for stealing Ken's wife, he is not condoning the gangster life, merely affirming the fact that other people's lives are bound up with one's own. Like the Toshiro Mifune/Charles Bronson western *Red Sun*, *The Yakuza* is an exploration of the West's empty individualism, not a serious look at the spiritual state of the East.

Mitchum was ideally cast. He later complained about 'that tedious romance', but his scenes with Kishi Keiko were among the best he'd ever done, suggesting a thinly-crusted vulnerability with a marvellously-judged mixture of gruff tenderness, embarrassment and fake nonchalance. His 'father-son' relationship with Richard Jordan was equally well-observed by both actors, while the tight-lipped respect he shared with Takakura Ken's unsmiling yakuza evoked echoes of many older films. Sitting there with his shotgun while Ken sliced up the opposition, he looked every inch the scout from *The Way West*, sadly watching the world go its uncontrollable way.

He carried the same wry semi-detachment into *Farewell,*

Going Home, 1971

181

My Lovely, the latest Hollywood attempt to cinematise Raymond Chandler. He was too old for the books' Marlowe, but the books were getting old too, and the film turned out a strange amalgam of nostalgia and up-dating.

Not everyone was pleased with this result. In the *Guardian* Derek Malcolm decided that while Altman had turned *The Long Goodbye* into 'something new and hopefully subversive', *Farewell, My Lovely* was nothing more than 'reverent if highly enjoyable pastiche'. This, though true as far as it went, failed to take changing times into account. *The Long Goodbye* subverted Bogart's Marlowe, the Hollywood knight errant, not Chandler's more ambivalent original, whereas *Farewell, My Lovely*, in truer seventies style, preferred the original ambivalence. In this respect the casting of Mitchum was a masterstroke. He would not have been idealistic enough for Bogart's world, nor innocent enough for the Marlowe which Altman thought necessary for corrupt LA. Mitchum's Marlowe may be the man doomed to wander the mean streets 'who is not himself mean', but he doesn't do it with any hope of eradicating meanness. Knight errants in the seventies neither solve important problems nor expose the system by failing to do so, they just save tomorrow's victim from today's victimisation.

Throughout the film Mitchum's Marlowe is more interested in DiMaggio's progress towards a baseball record than he is in the case. The record will be a real achievement, solving the riddle of Velma's disappearance will be just one small battle won in a losing war. The first few seconds of the film say it all: Marlowe finds an errant teenage girl for her parents, only to be ignored by them and kneed in the balls by her. He's just a social worker distributing elastoplast.

The original story has been shorn of many of its characters, but the plot remains as incomprehensible as ever. Much of the original dialogue has been retained, and it's as sharp as it was in 1940. Charlotte Rampling is as alluring as Velma should be, a sort of Lauren Bacall on heat. The photography by John Alonzo has the same beautiful amber haze which he brought to *Chinatown*.

Mitchum is a convincing Marlowe, despite the age discrepancy and the inevitable comparisons with those who had preceded him in the role. It was nearly thirty years since he'd last played a fully-fledged private eye, but the differences between Jeff Bailey in *Out of the Past* and his Marlowe were not particularly marked. This Marlowe is no brighter than Bailey, spending the whole film doggedly getting things wrong, though he does seem more wary of the *femme fatale*—he's 'old-fashioned from the waist up', he tells her—and he's definitely more conscious that other people exist. Indeed, the closing scene of *Farewell, My Lovely*, with Marlowe taking his hard-gotten earnings to the grieving widow of one of the villain's victims, teeters on the verge of sentimentality. He may still think the world's a cesspit, but like Eddie Coyle and Harry Kilmer he's grown more flexible with age. When people are bleeding they need elastoplasts.

9 Tequila Twilight

Left to right: Paul Sorvino, Bruce Dern, Jason Miller, Robert Mitchum, Stacy Keach and Martin Sheen in *That Championship Season*, 1982

'An old whore doesn't screw for fun.'

(Mitchum, 1977)

MITCHUM GREETED the critics' appreciation of his Marlowe in characteristic style: 'There was talk about my great work—*they* called it that—in *Farewell, My Lovely*. But every once in a while they gotta say something, just to acknowledge you're still around and kicking.' Over the years his relationship with the critics had not been particularly difficult, for the simple reason that he'd refused to take them seriously. On one of the few occasions, in 1983, that he did choose to hit back, it was simply to accuse them of making judgements without knowing all the facts. They'd criticise the actor when he was only following orders. 'They should write the director's instructions on the edge of the screen,' he noted sarcastically.

The journalists who followed him around off-screen

One Shoe Makes It Murder, CBS TV

received shorter shrift. They never seemed to be troubled by facts or the lack thereof, glibly twisting the former and making up for the latter with their imaginations. Mitchum once recounted how he was accosted by an English journalist in New York, who insisted on dragging a criticism of London out of him. Mitchum kept saying that London was one of his favourite cities, that there was nothing he disliked about it, but the journalist was persistent—surely there was something the actor would change if he could. Dredging his mind for an answer that would get rid of the scribe, Mitchum eventually said that he'd make the airport closer to the city. Catching the story weeks later he read the following: 'I finally tracked down cinema star Robert Mitchum . . . "What do you think of London?" I inquired. "I think they ought to move it closer to the airport," the burly Yank replied.'

But it wasn't only journalists and bad publicity that he had to worry about. During the shooting of *Going Home* a dog suddenly ran wild, biting one man and attacking the police officer who went to check whether it had had a rabies shot. The cop shot the dog. By that evening the story was going round that Mitchum had stepped in and violently admonished him for doing so. There was only one flaw in this story—Mitchum had been 500 miles away when the incident took place.

Interviewers have had mixed experiences with the actor over the years, the warmness of the welcome they received presumably depending on Mitchum's mood and how he took to the individual in question. A *Sunday Times* man who, in his own words, 'asked, deferentially, for a few words' was greeted with a stony 'frankly, I'd rather go for a piss'. Three hours later he tried again, and Mitchum was slightly more forthcoming. 'Frankly, I'd keep reporters off the set,' he said, 'it's like an operating theatre. Reporters contaminate the patient.'

The film in question was *The Big Sleep*, and the reporter duly asked Mitchum if he'd read the book. He hadn't, he said. 'Should I have read it? Would I get a better report card?' When a radio interviewer told him that the 1990s were coming he replied, 'That's deep, thanks for telling me.'

Some reporters, most notably Roderick Mann and Mike Tomkies, have interviewed him at regular intervals over the years, and seem to have gotten on well with him. The two men who interviewed him for *Rolling Stone*, Grover Lewis in 1973 and Robert Ward in 1983, both had an interesting time. Lewis, who interviewed him on the *Eddie Coyle* set, managed to draw Mitchum out on his early life, his writing and the bust, but failed to elicit any comments on his movie career, and much of the piece consisted of interviews with others involved in the film. Robert Ward did succeed in getting him to talk about films, and also had the temerity to suggest that Mitchum didn't need another drink, whereupon he was treated to a demonstration of the actor's head-butting technique. When the two said a fond farewell in a première lobby Mitchum quietly wished Ward luck with his writing, smiled, and then shouted 'What? Five Hundred Dollars? You want to go to a motel with me? Jesus Christ, man, what kind of guy do you think I am?'

Carrie Rickey, interviewing him for the *Village Voice*, found the same blend of ageing roué and kindly uncle. He told her she'd have to be 'nude between the sheets and wearing a false moustache' for the interview, and ended up teaching her a self-defence technique.

His definitive interview, however, was given to Bart Mills, also on the set of *Eddie Coyle*. 'I figure my presence is extraneous in an interview,' he said. No was always as good an answer as yes. 'If I say yes it becomes a complicated answer.' In any case, 'it's always published whether I say it or not'.

He at least understood the press; his fans continued to bemuse him. He still found it terrifying when he was recognised in a public place: 'I can't think that many people all headed in your direction mean you well, they can't be anything but a lynch mob or covering up for a pickpocket. They must have better things to do . . .' The same applied to autograph hunters. 'I don't know why people collect film stars' signatures—unless it's because they're free. In most places one goes they can't even read.'

On location for *Breakthrough* he found his Austrian fans particularly enthusiastic. 'I've never seen anything like it,' he told Roderick Mann. 'I guess they haven't seen too many celebrities around here since Hitler left. People dart from darkened buildings as I pass, thrusting sheaves of paper at me to sign. "The Zoo's that way" I say, but they refuse to quit. Even when I write "Get off my back, Wolfgang" it makes no difference. And they keep pestering me for pictures. It seems European stars carry pictures around with them for the fans. Me—nothing. So they stare at me as though my rear-end was on fire.'

'Hell, if one of my movies pulls people in out of the rain I say: OK—we fooled 'em again,' he said in 1977, damning both the movies and the fans in one neat sentence. After *Farewell, My*

Overleaf: With Victoria Tennant in *The Winds of War*, ABC TV

Lovely he continued his search for the ideal movie, which he defined as 'a boudoir comedy where I get to bed with lots of naked ladies', and filled in time with a couple of cameo roles. These had an appealing time/money ratio. He remembered how he'd used 'to watch actors like Claude Rains come on set with their little paper bags and two days later they picked up the loot and left. Thirty-two days later I was still there.'

Cameos, of course, came in all sizes. The makers of *Midway* initially wanted him to take a large one. 'They wanted me to play General Fletcher,' he told Roger Ebert. 'Ten weeks work. "Sorry," I said, "I can't spare the time." Then they have a role that's five weeks long. That's too long too. Finally they call me up and offer me a role as Bull Halsey. "How long?" I ask. "One day," they say, "and he's in a hospital bed." "I can just about handle that," I said.'

Actually he has three scenes in *Midway*, two in the flesh and one in the form of a photograph passed around by the Japanese High Command. It looks suspiciously like an old studio publicity shot, and one keeps expecting Yamamoto to bring a Jane Russell pic out of his folder. He doesn't, and the Japanese lose the battle for the second time.

Mitchum's role in *The Last Tycoon* was larger, but not much so. He played studio head Pat Brady, the mentor and eventual rival of Robert De Niro's Monroe Stahr. 'Good but dull', was Mitchum's verdict on the film, but he'd got 'ten days work and to wear a suit and to speak with some authority'. He and the other older actor don't seem to have been impressed by the time De Niro took to get ready for scenes, and one of them, Ray Milland, reportedly complained to director Kazan that they'd never been given so much time in their day. Kazan told him just to say his lines, 'I've got enough trouble with him.'

Mitchum also observed that Kazan had De Niro wander round the studio watching the executives to help him understand his part. 'What he hoped to learn from those cobras I'll never know. Kazan kept saying: "I'm worried. I've got this nude scene to direct with De Niro and Ingrid Boulting." "What are you worrying about?" I said, "being able to tell them apart?"'

He was back in the leading role for *The Amsterdam Kill*, an international thriller long on nations and short on thrills. He played an ex-narcotics agent who manages, after being pounded half to death by multinational gorillas, to smash a racket and expose the guilty man inside the agency. The

The Winds of War, ABC TV

filming was not one of his most pleasant experiences; it was 'like entering a motor race and finding they've fitted you with re-treads. For one thing the director is deaf. And I don't think he ever worked with live actors before. "Oh yes he has," they keep telling me, "he worked with Bruce Lee." "That's what I mean," I say, "that's what I mean" . . . In one of the scenes they have me in a canal. Have you ever seen those canals? They're filthy. All those houseboats spewing out their garbage. And there I am, up to my neck in it. I had to have a tetanus shot as a precaution. Not typhoid, of course, because then I might have broken out in a sweat and held up production.'

He stayed in Europe to make an Anglicised version of *The Big Sleep* with director-producer Michael Winner. Asked about this film Mitchum called it 'just bullshit', and for once he couldn't be accused of exaggeration. Despite the unwelcome novelty of its British settings the film sticks far too closely to the original, creating constant, unflattering comparisons. Mitchum is still a good Marlowe, but this Chandlerisation has none of Chandler's atmosphere, and the never-ending procession of well-known faces in small roles effectively destroys any sense of reality.

The bad run continued with *Matilda*, a comedy about a boxing kangaroo. Elliot Gould had the central role as the kangaroo's trainer, with Mitchum playing a crusading journalist out to expose corruption in the boxing business. There are a few funny moments, but the kangaroo—or rather the man inside the kangaroo suit—is singularly unconvincing and not very sympathetic. When the villians decide to destroy its balance by cutting off its tail they seem almost like heroes.

Mitchum's last seventies film was *Breakthrough*, a sequel to the excellent *Cross of Iron*. War movies have not been in fashion for several years, and the latter film's success was largely due to its unusual Eastern Front setting and the direction of Sam Peckinpah. *Breakthrough* had the same German 'hero', Sergeant Steiner, back on more familiar 'Western Front' territory, and director Andrew V. McLaglen could make nothing original of it. The $8 million budget went on the stars—Burton, Mitchum, Steiger and Jurgens—and the staging of tank battles. Mitchum's American major didn't have much to do.

As the decade turned he seemed to be settling for such roles—larger than cameos but smaller than those he'd been used to. In *Agency*, a Canadian-produced thriller, he played the villain, an advertising tycoon who takes to inserting subliminal political messages in his firm's commercials. Lee Majors played the copywriter who sets out to stop him, Valerie Perrine the love interest. But despite an interesting idea, and good performances from all the principals the film proved unexceptional. Like *Breakthrough* it had a severely limited commercial release.

That Championship Season was both a bigger picture and Mitchum's first non-gorilla movie since *The Yakuza* eight years earlier. It started life as a successful Broadway play, and was adapted for the screen by its writer Jason Miller. The cast, comprising Mitchum, Bruce Dern, Martin Sheen, Paul Sorvino and Stacy Keach, was exceptionally strong.

The story concerns five men who, twenty years earlier, had shared a sporting triumph. Four of them had been in the High School championship basketball team, the other (Mitchum) had been their coach. Now Dern is the city mayor, Keach an educational chief and the mayor's right-hand man, Sorvino a successful businessman who supports the mayor in return for favours, Sheen an alcoholic writer. Each year, usually minus the writer, they meet to celebrate the anniversary of their triumph.

This year it coincides with an upcoming mayoral election, and the strains imposed by Dern's likely defeat are causing cracks in their solidarity. As the evening proceeds and the booze flows all their skeletons come tumbling out of the closets, until all that remains is the memory of that now-distant triumph. Derek Malcolm thought that the film's conclusion, 'which suggests that if all the boys pull together like they did for the championship, the basketball game of life will be won', was an objectionable compromise, but for once he seems to have missed the point. This conclusion is so patently false that it becomes the last twist of the knife—even spilling out each other's hearts can teach this lot nothing about life. *That Championship Season* is as bleak a picture of middle America as could be imagined.

Before and after making this, his best film for some time, Mitchum finally began working for TV. He found it faster than movie-making—'you can get a double-hernia just checking the script'—but believed that TV was getting more 'specific' as the movies became more 'generalised, appealing to the Lowest Common Denominator'. 'TV will be OK,' he added, 'if they don't pay attention to those Moral Majority nuts, as they bill themselves.'

His first experience with the medium was not particularly happy. Signed to play Juan Peron in a TV movie of the dictator's life, he found himself up against Faye Dunaway's tem-

Overleaf: With Eric Stoltz (*left*) and Lance Kerwin in *A Killer in the Family*, ABC TV

195

perament. 'I have to take a long walk when she gets on my nerves—or I'd wind up dumping her on her derrière,' he reportedly said. Eventually he did take a long walk, right off the project.

He appeared in *One Shoe Makes It Murder*, a routine thriller with Angie Dickinson, and *A Killer in the Family*, an 'ABC Theatre' production, before signing on the dotted line for the TV serialisation of Herman Wouk's epic novel of World War II, *The Winds of War*. He cited the money—reportedly $600,000—as his prime motivation, but by the time filming ended he was not so sure. 'Considering the time I put into it, my pay works out at about $2.37 an hour. I could have done better picking potatoes. The most memorable moment of the entire thirteen months was the day I finished.'

Much the same could be said for the serial itself, an almost endless chunk of history-as-soap. Stephen Harvey, reviewing it for *Film Comment*, noted Mitchum's impression of a turtle doing its impression of John Wayne, and cracked the code of his overall performance: 'one dim blink means mild irritation or a faint itch of desire; four means Pearl Harbour has been sunk or his son is missing off Manila; seven means he's hung over.'

Mitchum was not in the best of health during the making of *The Winds of War*, and once more there was talk of retirement. For some time he had been telling interviewers how 'demeaning' it was to work at his age, and how after the series was finished he would 'rape . . . I go down to Mexico for the raping season.'

There were certainly no signs of him taking movies any more seriously as he got older, though he was prepared to talk seriously about how unserious they were. 'People,' he thought, 'make too much of acting. You are not helping anyone like being a doctor or even a musician. In the final analysis, you have exalted no one but yourself.' The young actors of today didn't seem to understand this, or chose to ignore it: 'These kids only want to talk about acting method and motivation; in my day all we talked about was screwing and overtime.'

Their dedication didn't seem to pay off where it mattered. 'I know production values are better,' he told Robert Ward, 'but are the scripts, are the pictures? . . . The thing is, it's a hell of a lot more work, and I don't see overall where the films are any better, really?' The older, less solemn approach worked just as well, if not better. He recalled how relaxed John Huston had always been, but insisted that Huston had known what he was doing. You didn't create art by saying to yourself, I'm going to go and create art. 'Where the hell would you be then? Look, take music. You can study it all you want, you can learn about time signatures, and you can know what legato means, and you can read it, and you can appreciate it, but if you haven't got an ear, if you're off-pitch, that's it. I've always had an ear.'

There's no doubt that Mitchum's 'ear', his enormous natural talent, has been the prime reason for his continued success over more than forty years. It seems all the more extraordinary then that his career, in most other respects, has closely paralleled that of Hollywood's most famous 'Method' actor, Marlon Brando. Both brought nonconformist personalities to Hollywood, both saw through the tinsel façade at an early stage in their careers, though it took Brando rather longer to admit 'defeat'. The directing of *One-Eyed Jacks* and the *Mutiny on the Bounty* fiasco destroyed his remaining illusions; Mitchum once claimed that he 'gave up being serious about pictures around the time I made a film with Greer Garson and she took 125 takes to say "no"'.

Both men possessed intelligence and awareness beyond that normally associated with Hollywood stars, and both came to see Hollywood's phoniness as symptomatic of a wider malaise. Brando defended the Red Indians, sided with America's blacks, worked for UNICEF and 'retired' to his Polynesian island, whereas Mitchum, who stayed in Hollywood's world, confined himself to the odd wistful utterance. After living with the Masai during the making of *Mister Moses* he asked 'if we think these people are primitive we had better take a good look at ourselves. Think of their free lives, then you tell me—who's civilised, them or us?' Years later he talked about visiting Kurdistan. 'They tell me the Kurds don't care if it's the year one or the year 5000. Those have got to be my kind of people.'

Because of their attitudes towards Hollywood and its movies, both men seemed to suffer a sense of absurdity where their work was concerned, and both have long been hyperconscious of living in the real shadow of an unreal stardom. Neither of them has found it easy to admit to a good performance. 'I often regret my good reviews,' Mitchum said once, 'because there is no point in doing something I know to be inferior and then I find I have come off the best in a film. Wouldn't you find that worrying?'

In an interview with Bill Davidson in 1962 he let himself go for once, startling his audience 'by reciting Wordsworth sonnets and by whistling the obscure classical music from which several Academy Award-winning musical scores had been stolen. Directly behind him, as he recited and whistled, was a large photograph of a depraved-looking Mitchum, hair askew, eyes at characteristic half-mast, whisky glass characteristically elevated towards the sensuous mouth . . . Mitchum caught me looking at the poster and abruptly terminated the sonnet he was reciting. "Forget about the poetry," he snapped. "That picture's the real me."'

Like Brando he has resolutely refused to laud his own talents, and by necessity both men have extended their self-depreciation to embrace the whole profession. When Brando asked 'Where are the great artists today?' in 1978 he was echoing Mitchum's 'Where are the real artists?' of 1967. Mitchum, typically terse, thought that 'today it's four-barrel carburettors and that's it', but it's hard to believe that he'd disagree with the sense, if not the fervour, of Brando's lengthier statement: 'We've somehow substituted craft for art and cleverness for craft. It's revolting! It's disgusting that people talk about art and they haven't got the right to use the word. It doesn't belong on anyone's tongue in this century. There are no artists. We are businessmen. We're merchants. There is no art.'

'You know perfectly well,' he added, 'that movie stars are not artists.' What they were, according to Mitchum, were 'masturbation images': 'up there on the screen you're thirty feet wide, your eyeball is six feet high, but it doesn't mean that you really amount to anything or have anything important to say.'

True, but it doesn't mean that you have nothing to say either, and it's impossible to escape the feeling, surveying Mitchum's long career, that he has wasted at least a part of his potential. Brando's answer, the sixties excepted, has been to make only those films which really interested him and those which paid for his extra-curricular projects. Mitchum's has been to hit the marks in movie after movie, and to turn his distaste into a long, and often highly amusing, joke. One can only guess how much sadness (if any) the clowning conceals. Sarah Miles thought he should never have been an actor, that he'd 'wasted a whole life on an image that isn't him', that it was 'really sad'. Mitchum, on one of those few occasions when the mask was allowed to slip, seemed almost to agree with her. 'Sometimes,' he said, 'I think I ought to go back and do at least one thing really well. But again, indolence will probably cause me to hesitate about finding a place to start. Part of that indolence perhaps is due to shyness because I'm a natural hermit. I've been in constant motion of escape all my life. I never really found the right corner to hide in.'

But overall he has no complaints. 'I got a great life out of the movies. I've been all over the world and met the most fantastic people. I don't really deserve all I've gotten. It's a privileged

200

life, and I know it.'

Few people have led such a full existence. He has known extreme poverty and extreme wealth, has been successful in his career and, it seems, as a husband and father. He has been praised for his writing, has even had hit records as a singer. He has indulged his love of literature, opera, horses and booze. He has made 101 movies which, for all his deprecation of them, have given and continue to give pleasure to millions. He has made a lot of people laugh.

The films keep coming. At the time of writing there are two more—*Maria's Lovers* with Nastassia Kinski, *The Ambassador* with Ellen Burstyn and Rock Hudson—awaiting release.

'I'll never retire,' he said in 1983. 'I have to work or I break out in terminal dandruff. I'm in the business because of ego. I have a deep need to impress my gardener.'

Gardeners everywhere should be impressed.

Filmography

Border Patrol (1943)
Director: Lesley Selander.
Producer: Harry Sherman.
Screenplay: Michael Wilson.
Star: William Boyd.

Hoppy Serves a Writ (1943)
Director: George Archainbaud.
Producer: Harry Sherman.
Screenplay: Gerald Geraghty.
Star: William Boyd.

The Leather Burners (1943)
Director: Joseph Henabery.
Producer: Harry Sherman.
Screenplay: Jo Pagano from Bliss
Lomax' story. Star: William Boyd.

The Human Comedy (1943)
Director/Producer: Clarence
Brown. Screenplay: Howard
Estabrook from William Saroyan's
novel. Stars: Mickey Rooney, James
Craig, Frank Morgan.

Aerial Gunner (1943)
Director: William Pine. Producers:
William Pine and William Thomas.
Screenplay: Maxwell Shane. Stars:
Chester Morris, Richard Arlen.

Follow the Band (1943)
Director: Jean Yarborough.
Producer: Paul Malvern.
Screenplay: Warren Wilson and
Dorothy Bennett from Richard
English's story. Stars: Eddie
Quillan, Mary Beth Hughes.

Colt Comrades (1943)
Director: Lesley Selander.
Producer: Harry Sherman.
Screenplay: Michael Wilson.
Star: William Boyd.

Bar 20 (1943)
Director: Lesley Selander.
Producer: Harry Sherman.
Screenplay: Morton Grant, Norman
Houston and Michael Wilson.
Star: William Boyd.

We've Never Been Licked (1943)
Director: John Rawlins. Producer:
Walter Wanger. Screenplay:
Norman Reilly Raine and Nick
Grindle from former's story. Stars:
Richard Quine, Ann Gwynne,
Martha O'Driscoll, Noah Beery Jr.

Corvette K-225 (1943)
Director: Richard Rosson.
Producer: Howard Hawks.
Screenplay: Lieutenant John
Rhodes Sturdy. Star: Randolph
Scott.

The Lone Star Trail (1943)
Director: Ray Taylor. Producer:
Oliver Drake. Screenplay: Oliver
Drake from Victor Halperin's story.
Stars: Johnny Mack Brown, Tex
Ritter.

Cry Havoc (1943)
Director: Richard Thorpe.
Producer: Edwin Knopf.
Screenplay: Paul Osborne from
Allan R. Kenward's play *Proof
Through the Night*. Stars: Margaret
Sullavan, Ann Sothern, Joan
Blondell, Fay Bainter, Marsha
Hunt, Ella Raines.

False Colors (1943)
Director: George Archainbaud.
Producer: Harry Sherman.
Screenplay: Bennett Cohen.
Star: William Boyd.

Minesweeper (1943)
Director: William Berke.
Producers: William Pine and
William Thomas. Screenplay:
Edward T. Lowe and Maxwell
Shane. Stars: Richard Arlen, Jean
Parker, Russell Hayden.

Beyond the Last Frontier (1943)
Director: Howard Bretherton.
Producer: Louis Gray. Screenplay:
John K. Butler and Morton Grant.
Stars: Eddie Dew, Smiley Burnette.

The Dancing Masters (1943)
Director: Malcolm St Clair.
Producer: Lee Marcus. Screenplay:
W. Scott Darling from George
Bricker's story. Stars: Stan Laurel,
Oliver Hardy.

Doughboys in Ireland (1943)
Director: Lew Landers. Producer:
Jack Fier. Screenplay: Howard J.
Green and Monte Brice. Stars:
Kenny Baker, Jeff Donnell, Lynn
Merrick.

Riders of the Deadline (1943)
Director: Lesley Selander.
Producer: Harry Sherman.
Screenplay: Bennett Cohen.
Star: William Boyd.

Gung Ho (1943)
Director: Ray Enright. Producer:
Walter Wanger. Screenplay: Lucien
Hubbard from factual account by
Captain W. S. LeFrancois. Stars:
Randolph Scott, Grace MacDonald,
Alan Curtis.

Mr Winkle Goes to War (1944)
Director: Alfred E. Green.
Producer: Jack Moss. Screenplay:
Waldo Salt, George Corey and
Louise Solomon from Theodore
Pratt's novel. Star: Edward G.
Robinson.

Girl Rush (1944)
Director: Gordon Douglas.
Producer: John Auer. Screenplay:
Robert E. Kent from story by
Laszlo Vadney and Aladar Laszlo.
Stars: Wally Brown, Alan Carey,
Frances Langford.

**Johnny Doesn't Live Here
Anymore** (1944)
Director: Joe May. Producer:
Maurice King. Screenplay: Philip
Yordan and John H. Kafka from
Alice Means Reeves' story. Stars:
Simone Simon, James Ellison,
William Terry.

Nevada (1944)
Director: Edward Killy. Producer:
Sid Rogell and Herman Scholm.
Screenplay: Norman Houston from
Zane Grey's story. Co-star: Anne
Jeffreys.

When Strangers Marry (1944)
Director: William Castle. Producer:
Maurice King. Screenplay: Philip
Yordan and Dennis Cooper from
George Moscov's story. Co-stars:
Dean Jagger, Kim Hunter.

Thirty Seconds over Tokyo (1944)
Director: Mervyn LeRoy.
Producer: Sam Zimbalist.
Screenplay: Dalton Trumbo from
novel by Captain Ted W. Lawson
and Robert Considine. Stars: Van
Johnson, Robert Walker, Phyllis
Thaxter, Spencer Tracy.

West of the Pecos (1945)
Director: Edward Killy. Producer:
Herbert Schlom. Screenplay:
Norman Houston from Zane Grey's
novel. Co-star: Barbara Hale.
Character: Pecos Smith.

The Story of GI Joe (1945)
Director: William A. Wellman.
Producer: Lester Cowan.
Screenplay: Leopold Atlas, Guy
Endore and Philip Stevenson from
Ernie Pyle's novel. Co-star: Burgess
Meredith. Character: Lieutenant
Walker.

Till the End of Time (1946)
Director: Edward Dmytryk.
Producer: Dore Schary. Screenplay:
Allen Rivkin from Niven Busch's
story 'They Dream of Home'.
Co-stars: Dorothy McGuire, Guy
Madison, Bill Williams. Character:
William Tabeshaw.

Undercurrent (1946)
Director: Vincente Minnelli.
Producer: Pandro S. Berman.
Screenplay: Edward Chodorov from
Thelma Stradel's story 'You Were
There'. Co-stars: Katharine
Hepburn, Robert Taylor.
Character: Michael Garroway.

The Locket (1946)
Director: John Brahm. Producer:
Bert Granet. Screenplay: Sheridan
Gibney. Co-stars: Laraine Day,
Brian Aherne, Gene Raymond.
Character: Norman Clyde.

Crossfire (1947)
Director: Edward Dmytryk.
Producer: Adrian Scott. Screenplay:
John Paxton from Richard Brooks'
novel *The Brick Foxhole*. Co-stars:
Robert Young, Robert Ryan.
Character: Sgt Peter Keeley.

Pursued (1947)
Director: Raoul Walsh. Producer:
Milton Sperling. Screenplay: Niven
Busch. Co-stars: Teresa Wright,
Judith Anderson, Dean Jagger.
Character: Jeb Rand.

Desire Me (1947)
Directors: George Cukor, Mervyn
LeRoy (both uncredited). Producer:
Arthur Hornblow Jr. Screenplay:
Marguerite Roberts and Zoe Akins
from Leonhard Frank's novel *Karl
and Anna*. Co-stars: Greer Garson,
Richard Hart. Character: Paul
Aubert.

Out of the Past (1947)
Director: Jacques Tourneur.
Producer: Warren Duff.
Screenplay: Geoffrey Holmes
(Daniel Mainwaring) from own
novel *Build My Gallows High*.
Co-stars: Jane Greer, Kirk Douglas,
Rhonda Fleming, Virginia Huston.
Character: Jeff Bailey.

Rachel and the Stranger (1948)
Director: Norman Foster.
Producer: Richard H. Berger.
Screenplay: Martin Rackin from
Howard Foster's novel *Rachel*.
Co-stars: Loretta Young, William
Holden. Character: Jim Fairways.

Blood on the Moon (1948)
Director: Robert Wise. Producers:
Sid Rogell and Theron Warth.
Screenplay: Lillie Hayward from
Luke Short's novel *Gunman's
Choice*. Co-stars: Barbara Bel
Geddes, Robert Preston, Tom
Tully, Walter Brennan. Character:
Jimmy Garry.

The Red Pony (1948)
Director/Producer: Lewis
Milestone. Screenplay: John
Steinbeck, from his own novel.
Co-stars: Myrna Loy, Louis
Calhern, Shepperd Strudwick, Peter
Miles. Character: Billy Buck.

The Big Steal (1949)
Director: Don Siegel. Producer:
Jack J. Gross. Screenplay: Geoffrey
Holmes (Daniel Mainwaring) and
Gerald Drayson Adams, from
Richard Wormser's story 'The Road
to Carmichael's'. Co-stars: Jane
Greer, William Bendix. Character:
Lieutenant Duke Halliday.

Holiday Affair (1949)
Director/Producer: Don Hartman.
Screenplay: Isobel Lennart from
John D. Weaver's story 'Christmas
Gift'. Co-stars: Janet Leigh,
Wendell Corey. Character: Steve
Mason.

Where Danger Lives (1950)
Director: John Farrow. Producer:
Irving Cummings Jr. Screenplay:
Charles Bennett from Leo Roslen's
story. Co-stars: Faith Domergue,
Claude Rains, Maureen O'Sullivan.
Character: Jeff Cameron.

My Forbidden Past (1951)
Director: Robert Stevenson.
Producers: Robert Sparks and Polan
Banks. Screenplay: Marion
Parsonner from Polan Banks' novel
Carriage Entrance. Co-stars: Ava
Gardner, Melvyn Douglas, Gordon
Oliver, Janis Carter. Character: Dr
Mark Lucas.

His Kind of Woman (1951)
Director: John Farrow. Producer:
Robert Sparks. Screenplay: Frank
Fenton and Jack Leonard. Co-stars:
Jane Russell, Vincent Price,
Raymond Burr. Character: Dan
Miller.

The Racket (1951)
Director: John Cromwell. Producer:
Edmund Grainger. Screenplay:
W. R. Burnett and William Wister
Haines from Bartlett Cormack's
play. Co-stars: Lizabeth Scott,
Robert Ryan. Character: Captain
Thomas McQuigg.

Macao (1952)
Director: Josef von Sternberg (and,
uncredited, Nicholas Ray).
Producer: Alex Gottlieb.
Screenplay: Bernard C. Shoenfield
and Stanley Rubin from Bob
Williams' story. Co-stars: Jane
Russell, William Bendix, Brad
Dexter, Gloria Grahame. Character:
Nick Cochran.

One Minute to Zero (1952)
Director: Tay Garnett. Producer:
Edmund Grainger. Screenplay:
Milton Krims and William Wister
Haines. Co-stars: Ann Blyth,
William Talman, Charles McGraw.
Character: Colonel Steve Janowski.

The Lusty Men (1952)
Director: Nicholas Ray. Producers:
Jerry Wald and Norman Krasna.
Screenplay: Horace McCoy and
David Dortort from Claude
Stanush's story. Co-stars: Susan
Hayward, Arthur Kennedy.
Character: Jeff McCloud.

Angel Face (1953)
Director: Otto Preminger.
Producer: Howard Hughes.
Screenplay: Frank Nugent and
Oscar Millard from Chester
Erskine's story. Co-star: Jean
Simmons. Character: Frank Jessup.

White Witch Doctor (1953)
Director: Henry Hathaway.
Producer: Otto Lang. Screenplay:
Ivan Goff and Ben Roberts from
Louise A. Stinedorf's novel.
Co-stars: Susan Hayward, Walter
Slezak. Character: Lonni Douglas.

Second Chance (1953)
Director: Rudolph Maté. Producer:
Sam Wiesenthal. Screenplay: Oscar
Millard and Sydney Boehm from
D. M. Marshman Jr's story. Co-stars.
Linda Darnell, Jack Palance.
Character: Russ Lambert.

She Couldn't Say No (1954)
Director: Lloyd Bacon. Producer:
Robert Sparks. Screenplay: D. D.
Beauchamp, William Bowers and
Richard Flourney, from the
former's story 'Enough for
Happiness'. Co-star: Jean Simmons.
Character: Doc.

River of No Return (1954)
Director: Otto Preminger.
Producer: Stanley Rubin.
Screenplay: Frank Fenton from
Louis Lanz's story. Co-stars:
Marilyn Monroe, Rory Calhoun,
Tommy Rettig. Character: Matt
Calder.

Track of the Cat (1954)
Director: William A. Wellman.
Producer: No credit. Screenplay:
A. I. Bezzerides from Walter Van
Tilburg Clark's novel. Co-stars:
Teresa Wright, Diana Lynn, Tab
Hunter, Beulah Bondi, Philip
Tonge, William Hopper. Character:
Curt Bridges.

Not as a Stranger (1955)
Director/Producer: Stanley Kramer.
Screenplay: Edna and Edward
Anhalt from Morton Thompson's
novel. Co-stars: Olivia de Havilland,
Frank Sinatra, Gloria Grahame,
Broderick Crawford, Charles
Bickford. Character: Lucas Marsh.

The Night of the Hunter (1955)
Director: Charles Laughton.
Producer: Paul Gregory.
Screenplay: James Agee from David
Grubb's novel. Co-stars: Shelley
Winters, Lillian Gish, Peter Graves,
Billy Chapin, Sally Jane Bruce.
Character: Harry Powell.

Man with the Gun (1955)
Director: Richard Wilson.
Producer: Samuel Goldwyn Jr.
Screenplay: N. B. Stone Jr. and
Richard Wilson. Co-star: Jan
Sterling. Character: Clint Tollinger.

Foreign Intrigue (1956)
Director/Producer: Sheldon
Reynolds. Screenplay: Sheldon
Reynolds from own story. Co-stars:
Genevieve Page, Ingrid Thulin.
Character: Dave Bishop.

Bandido! (1956)
Director: Richard Fleischer.
Producer: Robert L. Jacks.
Screenplay: Earl Felton. Co-stars:
Ursula Theiss, Gilbert Roland,
Zachary Scott. Character: Richard
Wilson.

Heaven Knows, Mr Allison (1957)
Director: John Huston. Producers:
Buddy Adler and Eugene Frenke.
Screenplay: John Lee Mahin and
John Huston from Charles Shaw's
novel. Co-star: Deborah Kerr.
Character: Corporal Allison.

Fire Down Below (1957)
Director: Robert Parrish.
Producers: Irving Allen and Albert
R. Broccoli. Screenplay: Irwin Shaw
from Max Catto's novel. Co-stars:
Rita Hayworth, Jack Lemmon.
Character: Felix.

The Enemy Below (1957)
Director/Producer: Dick Powell.
Screenplay: Wendell Mayes from
Commodore D. A. Rayner's novel.
Co-stars: Curt Jurgens. Character:
Captain Murrell.

Thunder Road (1958)
Director: Arthur Ripley. Producer:
Robert Mitchum. Screenplay:
James Atlee Phillips and Walter
Wise from Robert Mitchum's story.
Co-stars: Gene Barry, Jacques
Aubuchon, James Mitchum.
Character: Lucas Doolin.

The Hunters (1958)
Director/Producer: Dick Powell.
Screenplay: Wendell Mayes from
James Salter's novel. Co-stars:
Robert Wagner, Richard Egan, May
Britt. Character: Major Cleve
Saville.

The Angry Hills (1959)
Director: Robert Aldrich. Producer:
Raymond Stross. Screenplay: A. I.
Bezzerides from Leon Uris' novel.
Co-stars: Stanley Baker, Gia Scala.
Character: Mike Morrison.

The Wonderful Country (1959)
Director: Robert Parrish. Producer:
Chester Erskine. Screenplay:
Robert Ardrey from Tom Lea's
novel. Co-stars: Julie London, Gary
Merrill, Pedro Armendariz.
Character: Martin Brady.

Home from the Hill (1960)
Director: Vincente Minnelli.
Producer: Edmund Grainger.
Screenplay: Harriet Frank Jr and
Irving Ravetch from William
Humphrey's novel. Co-stars:
Eleanor Parker, George Peppard,
George Hamilton, Luana Patten,
Everett Sloane, Anne Seymour.
Character: Captain Wade Hunnicut.

The Sundowners (1960)
Director: Fred Zinnemann.
Producer: Gerry Blattner.
Screenplay: Isobel Lennart from
Jon Cleary's novel. Co-stars:
Deborah Kerr, Peter Ustinov,
Glynis Johns. Character: Paddy
Carmody.

The Night Fighters (1960)
Director: Tay Garnett. Producer:
Raymond Stross. Screenplay:
Robert Wright Campbell from
Arthur Roth's novel *A Terrible
Beauty*. Co-stars: Ann Heywood,
Dan O'Herlihy, Cyril Cusack,
Richard Harris. Character: Dermot
O'Neill.

The Grass is Greener (1960)
Director/Producer: Stanley Donen.
Screenplay: Hugh and Margaret
Williams from their own play.
Co-stars: Cary Grant, Deborah
Kerr, Jean Simmons. Character:
Charles Delacro.

The Last Time I Saw Archie
(1961)
Director/Producer: Jack Webb.
Screenplay: William Bowers.
Co-stars: Jack Webb, Martha Hyer,
France Nuyen. Character: Archie
Hall.

Cape Fear (1962)
Director: J. Lee Thompson.
Producer: Sy Bartlett. Screenplay:
James R. Webb from John D.
MacDonald's novel *The
Executioners*. Co-stars: Gregory
Peck, Polly Bergen, Lori Martin,
Martin Balsam, Telly Savalas.
Character: Max Cady.

The Longest Day (1962)
Directors: Andrew Marton, Ken
Annakin, Bernhard Wicki.
Producer: Darryl F. Zanuck.
Screenplay: Cornelius Ryan from
his own book. Co-stars: Almost
everybody. Character:
Brigadier-General Norman Cota.

Two for the Seesaw (1962)
Director: Robert Wise. Producer:
Walter Mirisch. Screenplay: Isobel
Lennart from William Gibson's
play. Co-star: Shirley MacLaine.
Character: Jerry Ryan.

The List of Adrian Messenger
(1963)
Director: John Huston. Producer:
Edward Lewis. Screenplay:
Anthony Veiller from Philip
MacDonald's novel. Stars: George
C. Scott, Dana Wynter.
Fellow-mystery celebrities: Tony
Curtis, Frank Sinatra, Burt
Lancaster, Kirk Douglas.
Character: Jim Slattery.

Rampage (1963)
Director: Phil Karlson. Producer:
William Fadiman. Screenplay:
Robert I. Holt and Marguerite
Roberts from Alan Caillon's novel.
Co-stars: Elsa Martinelli, Jack
Hawkins, Sabu. Character: Harry
Stanton.

Man in the Middle (1964)
Director: Guy Hamilton. Producer:
Walter Seltzer. Screenplay: Keith
Waterhouse and Willis Hall from
Howard Fast's novel *The Winston
Affair*. Co-stars: France Nuyen,
Barry Sullivan, Trevor Howard,
Keenan Wynn, Sam Wanamaker.
Character: Lieutenant-Colonel
Barney Adams.

What a Way to Go! (1964)
Director: J. Lee Thompson.
Producer: Arthur P. Jacobs.
Screenplay: Betty Comden and
Adolph Green from Gwen Davis'
story. Co-stars: Shirley MacLaine,
Paul Newman, Dean Martin, Gene
Kelly, Bob Cummings, Dick Van
Dyke. Character: Rod Anderson.

Mister Moses (1965)
Director: Ronald Neame. Producer:
Frank Ross. Screenplay: Charles
Beaumont and Monja
Danischewsky from Max Catto's
novel. Co-stars: Carroll Baker, Ian
Bannon. Character: Joe Moses.

The Way West (1967)
Director: Andrew V. McLaglen.
Producer: Harold Hecht.
Screenplay: Ben Maddow and Mitch
Linderman from A. B. Guthrie Jr's
novel. Co-stars: Kirk Douglas,
Richard Widmark. Character: Dick
Summers.

El Dorado (1967)
Director/Producer: Howard Hawks.
Screenplay: Leigh Brackett from
Harry Brown's novel *The Stars in
Their Courses*. Co-stars: John
Wayne, James Caan, Arthur
Hunnicut, Charlene Holt.
Character: J. P. Harrah.

Anzio (1968)
Director: Edward Dmytryk.
Producer: Dino D. Laurentiis.
Screenplay: Harry A. L. Craig from
Wynford Vaughan-Thomas' novel.
Co-stars: Peter Falk, Earl Holliman.
Character: Dick Ennis.

Five Card Stud (1968)
Director: Henry Hathaway.
Producer: Hal B. Wallis.
Screenplay: Marguerite Roberts
from Ray Gaulden's novel *Glory
Gulch*. Co-stars: Dean Martin,
Roddy McDowall, Inger Stevens.
Character: Jonathan Rudd.

Villa Rides (1968)
Director: Buzz Kulik. Producer:
Ted Richmond. Screenplay: Robert
Towne and Sam Peckinpah from
William Douglas Lansford's novel
Pancho Villa. Co-stars: Yul
Brynner, Charles Bronson.
Character: Lee Arnold.

Secret Ceremony (1968)
Director: Joseph Losey. Producers:
John Heyman and Norman Priggen.
Screenplay: George Tabori from
Marco Denevi's story. Co-stars: Liz
Taylor, Mia Farrow, Peggy
Ashcroft. Character: Albert.

Young Billy Young (1969)
Director: Burt Kennedy. Producer:
Max E. Youngstein. Screenplay:
Burt Kennedy from Will Henry's
novel *Who Rides With Wyatt*.
Co-stars: Angie Dickinson, Robert
Walker, David Carradine.
Character: Ben Kane.

The Good Guys and the Bad Guys
(1969)
Director: Burt Kennedy.
Production/Screenplay: Ronald M.
Cohen and Dennis Shryack.
Co-stars: George Kennedy, David
Carradine, Tina Louise, Martin
Balsam. Character: James Flagg.

Ryan's Daughter (1970)
Director: David Lean. Producer:
Anthony Havelock-Allan.
Screenplay: Robert Bolt. Co-stars:
Sarah Miles, Trevor Howard, John
Mills, Christopher Jones. Character:
Charles Shaughnessy.

Going Home (1971)
Director/Producer: Herbert B.
Leonard. Screenplay: Lawrence B.
Marcus. Co-stars: Brenda Vaccaro,
Jan-Michael Vincent. Character:
Harry Graham.

The Wrath of God (1972)
Director/Producer: Ralph Nelson.
Screenplay: Ralph Nelson from
James Graham's novel. Co-stars:
Rita Hayworth, Frank Langella,
Ken Hutchison, Victor Buono.
Character: Van Horne.

The Friends of Eddie Coyle (1973)
Director: Peter Yates. Producer:
Paul Monash. Screenplay: Paul
Monash from George V. Higgins'
novel. Co-stars: Peter Boyle, Steven
Keats, Richard Jordan, Alex Rocco.
Character: Eddie Coyle.

The Yakuza (1975)
Director/Producer: Sydney Pollack.
Screenplay: Paul Schrader and
Robert Towne from Leonard
Shrader's story. Co-stars: Takakura
Ken, Brian Keith, Richard Jordan,
Kishi Keiko, Herb Edelman.
Character: Harry Kilmer.

Farewell, My Lovely (1975)
Director: Dick Richards.
Producers: George Pappas and Jerry
Bruckheimer. Screenplay: David
Zelag Goodman from Raymond
Chandler's novel. Co-stars:
Charlotte Rampling, John Ireland,
Sylvia Miles, Harry Dean Stanton,
Jack O'Halloran, Anthony Zerbe.
Character: Philip Marlowe.

Midway (1976)
Director: Jack Smight. Producer:
Walter Mirisch. Screenplay: Donald
S. Sandford. Co-stars: Charlton
Heston, Henry Fonda, James
Coburn, Glenn Ford, Hal
Holbrook, Toshiro Mifune, Cliff
Robertson, Robert Wagner.
Character: Admiral Halsey.

The Last Tycoon (1976)
Director: Elia Kazan. Producer:
Sam Spiegel. Screenplay: Harold
Pinter from F. Scott Fitzgerald's
novel. Co-stars: Robert De Niro,
Tony Curtis, Jeanne Moreau, Jack
Nicholson, Donald Pleasance, Ray
Milland, Dana Andrews, Ingrid
Boulting. Character: Pat Brady.

The Amsterdam Kill (1977)
Director: Robert Clouse. Producer:
Andre Morgan. Screenplay: Robert
Clouse and Gregory Tiefer.
Co-stars: Bradford Dillman,
Richard Egan. Character: Quinlan.

The Big Sleep (1978)
Director/Producer: Michael
Winner. Screenplay: Michael
Winner from Raymond Chandler's
novel. Co-stars: Sarah Miles,
Richard Boone, Candy Clark, Joan
Collins, Edward Fox, John Mills,
Oliver Reed, James Stewart.
Character: Philip Marlowe.

Matilda (1978)
Director: Daniel Mann. Producer:
Albert S. Ruddy. Screenplay:
Albert S. Ruddy and Timothy
Galfas from Paul Gallico's novel.
Co-stars: Elliot Gould, Harry
Guardino. Character: Duke
Parkhurst.

Breakthrough (1980)
Director: Andrew V. McLaglen.
Producers: Wolf C. Hartwig and
Hubert Lukowski. Screenplay:
Tony Williamson. Co-stars: Richard
Burton, Rod Steiger, Helmut
Griem, Curt Jurgens. Character:
Colonel Rogers.

Agency (1981)
Director: George Kaczender.
Producer: Robert Lantos.
Screenplay: Noel Hynd from Paul
Gottlieb's novel. Co-stars: Valerie
Perrine, Lee Majors. Character:
Ted Quinn.

That Championship Season (1982)
Director: Jason Miller. Producers:
Menahem Golan and Yoram
Globus. Screenplay: Jason Miller
from his own play. Co-stars: Bruce
Dern, Martin Sheen, Stacy Keach,
Paul Sorvino. Character: Coach
Delaney.

The Ambassador (1984)
Director: J. Lee Thompson.
Producers: Menahem Golan and
Yoram Globus. Screenplay: Ronald
M. Cohen. Co-stars: Ellen Burstyn,
Rock Hudson, Fabio Testi, Donald
Pleasance.

Maria's Lovers (1984)
Director: Andrei Konchalovsky.
Producers: Lawrence
Taylor-Mortorff and Bosko
Djordjevic. Screenplay: Gerard
Brach, Andrei Konchalovsky, Paul
Zindel and Marjorie David.
Co-stars: Nastassia Kinski, John
Savage, Keith Carradine.